STORIES TOLD

CEMETERY ICONOLOGY

A Manual for Genealogy Research

Gaylord Cooper

Motes Books

NON-FICTION

STORIES TOLD IN STONE
Cemetery Iconology: A Manual for Genealogy Research

by
Gaylord Cooper

ISBN 978-1-934894-19-4
NON-FICTION

© 2009 - MotesBooks Inc
All Rights Reserved.

EDITED BY JASON HOWARD
DESIGNED BY EK LARKEN

IMAGE CREDITS
JASON HOWARD: *4, 8, 24, 36, 51, 53, 54, 58, 63, 66, 70, 73, 82, 96, 109, 118*
EK LARKEN: *front & back covers, 1, 3, 6, 11, 15, 17, 19, 21, 23, 30, 31, 33, 37, 45, 47, 48, 50, 56, 59, 60, 61, 68, 69,
71, 72, 74, 76, 77, 78, 79, 81, 82, 83, 84, 85, 86, 87, 88, 89, 90, 92, 93, 95, 96, 97,
102, 104, 105, 106, 107, 111, 112, 114, 116, 119, 120, 121, 123, 124, 125, 126, 127*
AUTHOR'S COLLECTION: *back cover portrait, 12, 69, 72, 80*
PORTLAND MUSEUM: *98*

Published by

Louisville, Kentucky

www.MOTESBOOKS.com

Author's Note

This manual is not intended simply to be read and discarded.
It is a workbook designed to be taken with you and used anytime you do research.
It will not be all you need to track down those elusive ancestors or their final resting places,
but it is a necessary item for your genealogy work kit.

Please remember to be kind to the gravestones and cemeteries.
They are open-air museums, repositories of history and the final resting place of your ancestors.
After all, ancestors are family.

Sources

Research sources for this manual include:

BOOKS

The Wars of Our Ancestors - Miguel Delibes (author), Agnes Moncy (translator)
Cleaning Masonry Burial Monuments - Ky. Historical Society Cemetery Preservation & Education Project
Field Guide #4: Cleaning Masonry Burial Monuments - Association of Gravestone Studies -
Tracy L. Coffing & Fred Oakley (authors)

WEBSITES

http://hawkshome.net/misc_items/events/epidemic_timeline.htm
www.usgennet.org/usa/ar/county/greene/olddiseases1.htm
http://en.wikipedia.org/wiki/List_of_epidemics
www.obcgs.com/rebels.htm
http://freepages.genealogy.rootsweb.ancestry.com/~kordyban/chart/relationship_chart.html
http://genealogy.about.com/library/free_charts/bl_pedigree.htm
www.familytreemagazine.com/upload/images/pdf/cemetery.pdf
www.searchgenealogy.net/GenealogyForms.html
http://misbach.org/pdfcharts

Chapters

Foreword - Dr. James Gifford 7

1   The History of Cemeteries & Gravestones 9

2   Identifying Your Ancestors 25

3   Finding A Cemetery 55

4   Stone Identification 67

5   Gravestone Weathering & Repair 93

6   TakingRubbings 101

Poem - "Stories" 126

Tools

Historic Diseases 13
Major Epidemics/Pandemics 22
Wars 31
Relationship Terms 32
Relationship Chart 34
Pedigree Chart 35
Family Group Sheet 38
Genealogy-Related Terms 40
Historic Occupations 48
Cemetery Worksheet 64
Cemetery Transcription Form 65
Symbols/Interpretations 71
Abbreviations On Gravestones 84
Visual Guide To Monuments 90
Gravestone Elements/Cemetery Vocabulary 105

Foreword

Social philosophers (and grumpy old men, like me) often bemoan the fact that Americans are spending more time on leisure pursuits and less time working. While many see these two factors in negative terms and criticize what they see as a do-less and self-absorbed society, there is a bright side to increasing leisure: some people use it positively and constructively. For example, in the last two decades millions of Americans have become almost obsessed with genealogical research.

At one time, the general public stereotyped genealogical research as the province of blue-haired old ladies in tennis shoes who haunted libraries and archives in pursuit of their forbears. Now genealogy is a hobby and intellectual pursuit for men and women of all ages and stations. The internet has become an invaluable tool for Americans in search of their ancestral roots, but other specialized research tools are emerging, too.

One is *Stories Told in Stone,* this workbook by Gaylord Cooper for genealogists of all skill levels who undertake cemetery iconography and gravestone interpretation. Researchers who spend time in cemeteries and graveyards confront a confusing array of carvings, monuments and statues. Cooper's workbook takes the mystery and the guesswork out of interpreting these icons and markers. This fine genealogical tool explains that these icons and symbols offer factual insight into ethnicity, religious affiliation, association membership, kinships, cause of death and even occupation.

Stories Told in Stone also enables genealogical researchers to interpret cemetery and graveyard icons within the historical context of their times. For example, the term "Cousin" was often used to describe any close relative or friend, and the designation of "Uncle" or "Aunt" may have denoted respect rather than blood kinship.

Stories Told in Stone will help you transform cemeteries and graveyards into open-air museums and archives. Good hunting, my friends!

JAMES M. GIFFORD, PH.D.
CEO & Senior Editor
Jesse Stuart Foundation

DECEMBER 19, 2008

CHAPTER 1

The History of
CEMETERIES & GRAVESTONES

Anyone who has conducted genealogical research ...

... has found that a significant amount of time is spent in cemeteries searching for graves of long-deceased ancestors.

The staggering array of motifs, carvings, statues and monuments can be overwhelming. Most of them, however, were not put there on a whim. Instead, they were carefully chosen, usually in an attempt to commemorate and reflect the thinking of the deceased.

Gravestones may indicate religious preference or beliefs. The carvings may display information about diseases from which the deceased may have died. Occupations and organizations they belonged to may be listed. The information often goes beyond what is documented in old records, giving us a sense of the real people, of their lives and loves and work and struggles. All we have to do is learn the language of the stones, to read and listen to the stories they have to tell us.

However, this can be tricky; the meaning of symbols sometimes changes over time. One should not view them through the eyes and thought processes of today. Instead, a local historical perspective should be adopted. An icon might have different meaning across regions of the country or world. Old diseases, relationship terms, abbreviations and initials cannot be read using modern thinking and understanding.

In short, *gravestone iconology* is the study of the various symbols, carvings, monuments, motifs and icons found in cemeteries. This knowledge is an important tool in the study of genealogy. The field includes historical and cultural attitudes regarding death and burial practices reflected on the gravestones themselves. Therefore, this is part science, part art, part history and, frankly, it is sometimes part tea-leaf reading, too. Often, interpreting a gravestone can come down to making an educated guess (the key word here being *educated*). However, gravestone icons most often share common meanings.

Iconography is image writing. A translation of a Greek term, it is the study of symbols depicted in works of art. Traditionally, those symbols are derived from a readily recognizable, common currency of cultural or religious experience. For example, a cross is a familiar shorthand symbol for Christianity; an obelisk is considered an emblem of dominance and, in western culture, can also refer to power over death or a connection between heaven and earth.

Similarly, *iconology* is the study, description, analysis and interpretation of icons. Historically, the term *icon* refers to a painted description of religious significance in western culture that has evolved to include any symbol that is widely recognized. The golden arches of McDonald's and the shape of a stop sign do not require words of explanation; the symbols themselves are easily identifiable almost everywhere.

Social convention historically deemed it necessary for gravestone icons to provide information associated with the deceased. Our modern ideas of simply selecting what is appealing without regard to meaning would have been a foreign one to our forebears. In order to understand the full story today, we must first look to the past.

The earliest gravestones were simply piles of rocks (called "cairns" in some places), a utilitarian design to both mark the grave and keep wild animals away. Superstitions of this time period also held that the dead could come back and haunt the living; people believed that the stones would keep their spirits in the ground. Ledger stones – large, flat slabs that covered the entire grave – became popular during the Middle Ages as a result of these beliefs.

Until the 1500s, gravestones were largely a luxury of the upper class. They became prevalent among the lower classes along with the birth of the Protestant religion, which emphasized the worth of the individual. The first such markers were simple, bearing only the name and age of the departed, along with the year of death.

In Europe, churchyards were the preferred burial place. Within those, the most favored sites were to the east, as close as possible to the church. In such a location, the dead would be assured the best view of the rising sun on the Day of Judgment. People of lesser distinction were buried on the south side, while the north corner was considered the devil's domain, reserved for stillborns, bastards and strangers unfortunate enough to die while passing through a town. Suicides, if they were buried in consecrated ground at all, were also usually deposited in the north end, although their corpses were not allowed to enter through the cemetery gates. Instead, they were passed over the top of the stone wall.

During the late Middle Ages, the pressure of space finally exorcised the devil from the north end of the churchyard to make room for more burials. Consequently, it soon became nearly impossible for the churchyards to hold the bodies of the dead. As the population of towns and cities exploded during the 1700s, a chronic shortage of space developed. The impact on the deceased was tremendous; the first solution was to simply pack the coffins more closely together. Later, the coffins were stacked on top of one another. Dirt was added to the graves, and often the piles of dirt and bodies rose higher than the bottom of the church doors. Walls were built around the churchyard to hide the graves in an attempt to contain the odor of the tightly-packed corpses. The churchyards were dank, odorous places full of disease, with the local water source sometimes running through it.

In Paris, the walls of the city cemetery collapsed, spilling bodies and bones into the street. The public outcry for reform led to new laws and a change in burial methods. The founding of the Pere-Lachaise Cemetery is considered to be the first "garden" cemetery.

The movement quickly spread to America, as the United States generally followed the European model of cemeteries. The first of these was Mount Auburn Cemetery in Cambridge, Massachusetts, which was consecrated in 1831. It featured an Egyptian-style gate and fence, as well as a Norman tower and granite chapel. Mount Auburn was planned as an oasis on the outskirts of the city and defined a new romantic version of the cemetery, complete with winding paths and a forested setting. The opposite of the overcrowded churchyard, it became an immediate success, giving rise to many other similar burial grounds in cities across the country. In fact, such sites became so popular that the public began using them as recreation areas, enjoying the shaded walkways and picnics on weekend afternoons. The garden cemetery inspired the American park movement and virtually created the field of landscape architecture.

It was then, during the Victorian Era, that mourning became a social institution. Entire industries sprang up to cater to the bereaved, offering special clothing and other materials that a proper mourner could not do without. Books were written on how to mourn, when to mourn, how long to mourn and what types of clothing in which to mourn.

Gravestone symbols evolved along with the styles of cemeteries. Carving elaborate icons on gravestones became the rage; the bereaved chose symbols that they thought described the deceased. Like the ancients, they gave symbolic meanings to virtually every flower, tree, shrub and object.

As time passed, people began adding more information and icons to gravestones, a direct result of new attitudes about death and the evolution of cemeteries. The morbid focus on death and the shortness and futility of life evolved into looking beyond death.

More sophisticated tools and methods of transportation also led to more intricate gravestone carvings. Skull-and-crossbones carvings (meaning "here lies death"), popular among the Puritans during the 17th and early 18th centuries, morphed first into a winged skull (called a "death's head") and then into cherubic winged angels during the 1700s. Urns and willow trees were popular symbols in the late 18th and early 19th centuries. Markers expressing themes of eternity, rebirth and the experience of the deceased became widely used in the mid-19th Century.

Technical and artistic advancements led to beautiful craftsmanship. But as with all new technologies, mistakes were sometimes made. Incorrect dates, relationships and even names occasionally appeared on grave markers. As the craft of carving was labor intensive and expensive, errors were typically ignored. The carver was usually reluctant to toss aside his time-consuming work, and mourners were not likely to add to their expense by purchasing a new gravestone.

Errors such as these have caused many headaches among genealogists. In addition, certain motifs, carvings and icons are the cause of much debate among experts in the field. Occasionally the symbols will be so personal that only family members know the meanings. However, such instances are rare.

Although simply reading and interpreting the symbols is an important part of gravestone iconology, the study encompasses much more, a good deal of which will be explored in this book, including: successfully identifying ancestors, locating cemeteries, stone identification, interpreting language and abbreviations, how to properly clean and repair gravestones and, finally, taking a rubbing.

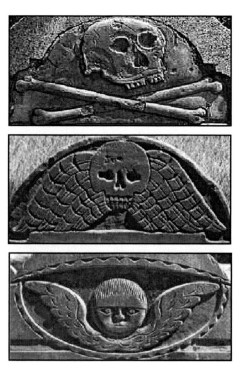

Glossary of Historic Diseases

Ablepsy - blindness

Ague - malarial fever

American plague - yellow fever

Anasarca - generalized massive edema

Aphonia - laryngitis

Aphtha - the infant disease "thrush"

Apoplexy - paralysis due to stroke

Asphycsia/Asphicsia/Asphyxia - cyanotic and lack of oxygen

Atrophy - wasting away or diminishing in size

Bad blood - syphilis

Bilious fever - typhoid, malaria, hepatitis or elevated temperature

Biliousness - jaundice associated with liver disease

Black plague - bubonic plague

Black fever - acute infection with high temperature and dark red skin lesions; high mortality rate

Black pox - smallpox manifested as dark bleeding beneath skin and membrane, causing it to fall away

Black vomit - vomiting old black blood due to ulcers or yellow fever

Blackwater fever - dark urine associated with high temperature and dehydration

Bladder in throat - diphtheria

Blood poisoning - bacterial infection; septicemia

Bloody flux - bloody stools

Bloody sweat - sweating sickness

Bone shave - sciatica

Brain fever - meningitis

Breakbone - dengue fever

Bright's disease - chronic inflammatory disease of kidneys

Bronze John - yellow fever

Bule - boil, tumor or swelling

Cachexy - malnutrition

Cacogastric - upset stomach

Cacospysy - irregular pulse

Caduceus - falling sickness or epilepsy

Camp fever – typhus or camp diarrhea

Canine madness - rabies, hydrophobia

Canker - ulceration of mouth or lips; herpes simplex

Catalepsy - seizures/trances

Catarrhal - nose and throat discharge from cold or allergy

Cerebritis - inflammation of cerebrum or lead poisoning

Chilblain - swelling of extremities caused by exposure to cold

Child bed fever - infection following birth of a child

Chin cough - whooping cough

Chlorosis - iron deficiency anemia

Cholecystitus - inflammation of the gall bladder

Cholelithasis - gallstones

Cholera - acute, severe and contagious diarrhea with intestinal lining sloughing

Cholera morbus - characterized by nausea, vomiting, abdominal cramps, elevated temperature

Chorea - disease characterized by convulsions, contortions and involuntary "dancing"

Cold plague - ague characterized by chills

Colic - an abdominal cramping

Congestive chills - malaria

Consumption - tuberculosis

Congestion - any collection of fluid in an organ, such as the lungs

Congestive chills - malaria with diarrhea

Congestive fever - malaria

Corruption - infection

Coryza - a cold

Costiveness - constipation

Cramp colic - appendicitis

Crop sickness - overextended stomach

Croup - laryngitis, diphtheria or strep throat

Cyanosis - dark skin color, lack of oxygen in blood

Cynanche - diseases of throat

Cystitis - inflammation of the bladder

Day fever - lasting one day; sweating sickness

Debility - lack of movement or staying in bed

Decrepitude - feebleness due to old age

Delirium tremens - hallucination due to alcoholism

Dengue - infectious fever endemic to East Africa

Dentition - cutting of teeth

Deplumation - tumor of the eyelids which causes hair loss

Diary fever - fever that lasts one day

Diptheria - contagious disease of the throat

Distemper - usually animal disease with malaise, discharge from nose and throat; anorexia

Dock fever - yellow fever

Dropsy - edema (swelling), often caused by kidney or heart disease

Dropsy of the brain - encephalitis

Dry bellyache - lead poisoning

Dyscrasy - abnormal body condition

Dysentery - inflammation of colon with frequent passage of mucous and blood

Dysorexy - reduced appetite

Dyspepsia - indigestion and heartburn

Dysury - difficulty in urination

Eclampsy - symptoms of epilepsy or convulsions during labor

Ecstasy - a form of catalepsy

Edema - nephrosis; swelling of tissues

Edema of lungs - congestive heart failure, a form of dropsy

Eel thing - erysipelas; fever and raised red patches on skin

Elephantiasis - a form of leprosy

Encephalitis - swelling of brain; sleeping sickness

Enteric fever - typhoid fever

Enterocolitis - inflammation of the intestines

Enteritis - inflations of the bowels

Epitaxis - nosebleed

Erysipelas - contagious skin disease, due to streptococci with vesicular bulbous lesions

Extravasted blood - rupture of a blood vessel

Falling sickness - epilepsy

Fatty liver - cirrhosis of liver

Fits - sudden attack or seizure of muscle activity

Flux - an excessive flow or discharge of fluid like hemorrhage or diarrhea

Flux of humour - circulation problems

French pox - syphilis

Gathering - a collection of pus

Glandular fever - mononucleosis

Great pox - syphilis

Green fever/sickness - anemia

Grippe/grip - influenza-like symptoms

Grocer's itch - skin disease caused by mites from sugar or flour

Heart sickness - condition caused by loss of salt from body

Heat stroke - body temperature elevates because of surrounding environment temperature and body does not perspire to reduce temperature; coma and death result if not reversed

Hectical complaint - recurrent fever

Hematemesis - vomiting blood

Hematuria - bloody urine

Hemiplegy - paralysis of one side of body

Hip gout - osteomylitis

Horrors - delirium tremens

Hydrocephalus - enlarged head; "water on the brain"

Hydropericardium - heart dropsy

Hydrophobia - rabies

Hydrothroax - dropsy in chest

Hypertrophic - enlargement of organ, such as the heart

Impetigo - contagious skin disease characterized by pustules

Inanition - physical condition resulting from lack of food

Infantile paralysis - polio

Intestinal colic - abdominal pain due to bad diet

Jail fever - typhus

Jaundice - condition caused by blockage of intestines

King's evil - tuberculosis of neck and lymph glands

Kruchhusten - whooping cough

Lagrippe - influenza

Lockjaw - tetanus or infectious disease affecting muscles of the neck and jaw; fatal in 8 days if untreated

Long sickness - tuberculosis

Lues disease - syphilis

Lues venera - venereal disease

Lumbago - back pain

Lung fever - pneumonia

Lung sickness - tuberculosis

Lying in - time of delivery of infant

Malignant sore throat - diphtheria

Mania - insanity

Marasmus - progressive wasting away of body; related to malnutrition

Membranous croup - diphtheria

Meningitis - inflammation of brain or spinal cord

Metritis - inflammation of uterus or purulent vaginal discharge

Miasma - poisonous vapors thought to infect the air

Milk fever - disease from drinking contaminated milk; infection developed after childbirth

Milk leg - postpartum thrombophlebitis

Milk sickness - disease from milk of cow that had eaten poisonous weeds

Mormal - gangrene

Morphew - scurvy blisters on the body

Mortification - gangrene of necrotic tissue

Myelitis - inflammation of the spine

Myocarditis - inflammation of heart muscles

Necrosis - mortification of bones or tissue

Nephrosis - kidney degeneration

Nepritis - inflammation of kidneys

Nervous prostration - extreme exhaustion resulting from headache

Neuralgia - nerve discomfort, typically in head or face

Nostalgia - homesickness

Palsy - paralysis or uncontrolled movement of muscles

Paroxysm - convulsion

Pemphigus - skin disease of watery blisters

Pericarditis - inflammation of heart

Peripneumonia - inflammation of lungs

Peritonotis - inflammation of abdominal area

Petechial fever - fever characterized by skin spotting

Phthiriasis - lice infestation

Phthisis - chronic wasting away; tuberculosis

Plague - an acute, febrile, highly-infectious disease with a high fatality rate

Pleurisy - pain in the chest area that is evident with each breath

Podagra - gout

Pott's disease - tuberculosis of spine

Puerperal exhaustion - death due to child birth

Puerperal fever - elevated temperature after childbirth

Puking fever - milk sickness

Putrid fever - diphtheria

Quinsy - tonsillitis

Remitting fever - malaria

Rheumatism - any disorder associated with pain in joints

Rickets - disease of skeletal system

Rose cold - hay fever or nasal symptoms of an allergy

Rottany fever - thought to refer to a child's disease

Rubeola - German measles

Sanguineous crust - scab

Scarletina - scarlet fever

Scarlet fever – disease characterized by red rash

Scarlet rash - roseola

Sciatica - rheumatism in the hips

Scirrhus - cancerous tumors

Scotomy - dizziness, nausea and dimness of sight

Scrivener's palsy - writer's cramp

Screws - rheumatism

Scrofula - tuberculosis of neck lymph glands; progresses slowly with abscesses and pistulas; young person's disease

Scrumpox - skin disease; impetigo

Scurvy - lack of vitamin C; results in symptoms of weakness, spongy gums and hemorrhages under skin

Septicemia - blood poisoning

Shakes - delirium tremens

Shaking - chills, ague

Shingles - viral disease with skin blisters

Ship fever - typhus

Siriasis - inflammation of the brain due to sun exposure

Sloes - milk sickness

Smallpox - contagious disease with fever and blisters

Softening of brain - result of stroke or hemorrhage in the brain, with an end result of the tissue softening in that area

Sore throat distemper - diphtheria or quinsy

Spanish influenza - epidemic influenza

Spasms - sudden involuntary contraction of muscle or group of muscles; convulsion

Spina bifida - deformity of spine

Spotted fever - typhus or meningitis

Sprue - tropical disease characterized by intestinal disorders and sore throat

St. Anthony's fire - infection; also known as erysipelas (bacteria-caused fever and skin areas that are bright red in appearance) or ergotism (poisoning caused by eating the fungus ergot, resulting in headache, vomiting, gangrene in fingers and toes)

St. Vitus's dance - ceaseless occurrence of rapid, complex, involuntary jerking movements (also called St. Vita's dance)

Stomatitis - inflammation of the mouth

Stranger's fever - yellow fever

Strangery - rupture

Sudor anglicus -sweating sickness

Summer complaint - diarrhea, usually in infants caused by spoiled milk

Sunstroke - uncontrolled elevation of body temperature due to environmental heat. Lack of sodium in the body is a predisposing cause

Swamp sickness - malaria, typhoid or encephalitis

Sweating sickness - infectious and fatal disease common to the U.K. in 15th Century

Tetanus -infectious fever characterized by high fever, headache and dizziness

Thrombosis - blood clot inside blood vessel

Thrush - childhood disease characterized by spots on mouth, lips and throat

Tick fever - Rocky Mountain spotted fever

Toxemia - eclampsia

Trench mouth - painful ulcers found along gum line, caused by poor nutrition and poor hygiene

Tussis convulsiva - whooping cough

Typhus - infectious fever characterized high fever, headache and dizziness

Variola - smallpox

Venesection - bleeding

Viper's dance - St. Vitus's (or St. Vita's) dance

Water on brain - enlarged head

White swelling - tuberculosis of the bone

Winter fever - pneumonia

Womb fever - infection of the uterus

Genealogical research often involves a detailed search for people who disappear from local records. This list of American epidemics may help in finding the cause of their disappearance from public records. One often can find the cause of death written on the gravestone itself.

1657	Boston	Measles
1687	Boston	Measles
1690	New York	Yellow Fever
1713	Boston	Measles
1729	Boston	Measles
1732-3	Worldwide	Influenza
1738	South Carolina	Smallpox
1739-40	Boston	Measles
1747	Connecticut, New York, South Carolina & Pennsylvania	Measles
1759	North America	Measles
1761	North America & West Indies	Influenza
1772	North America	Measles
1775	North America	Unknown epidemic (especially in Northeast)
1775-6	Worldwide	Influenza
1783	Dover, DE	"Extremely fatal" bilious disorder
1788	Philadelphia & New York	Measles
1793	Vermont	Influenza
1793	Philadelphia	Yellow Fever
1793	Harrisburg & Middletown, PA	Many unexplained deaths
1794-8	Philadelphia	Yellow Fever
1803	New York	Yellow Fever
1820-3	Nationwide	Unknown "Fever" (started at Schuylkill River and spread across the country)
1822	New York & New Orleans	Yellow Fever
1831-2	Nationwide	Asiatic Cholera: brought by English immigrants
1832	New York and other major cities	Cholera
1832	New Orleans	Asiatic Cholera
1833	Columbus	Cholera
1834	New York	Cholera
1837	Philadelphia	Typhus
1841	Nationwide	Yellow Fever (especially severe in the South)
1847	New Orleans	Yellow Fever
1847-8	Worldwide	Influenza
1848-50	New York, New Orleans & North America	Cholera
1850	Nationwide	Yellow Fever

1850	Alabama, New York	Cholera
1850-1	North America	Influenza
1851	Coles Co., IL, The Great Plains and Missouri	Cholera
1852	Nationwide	Yellow Fever
1853	New Orleans	Yellow Fever
1855	Nationwide	Yellow Fever
1857-9	Worldwide	Influenza
1860-1	Pennsylvania	Smallpox
1865-73	Philadelphia, New York, Boston, New Orleans, Baltimore, Memphis, Washington, D.C.	Series of recurring epidemics of Smallpox, Cholera, Typhus, Typhoid, Scarlet Fever, Yellow Fever
1873-5	North America and Europe	Influenza
1878	New Orleans, Memphis	Yellow Fever
1885	Chicago	Water-borne disease
1885	Plymouth, PA	Typhoid
1886	Jacksonville, FL	Yellow Fever
1895	Washington, D.C.	Malaria
1898	Cuba (US soldiers in Sp-Am War)	Yellow Fever (5 times more deaths than from battle)
1900	Galveston	Cholera
1902	Alabama	Measles
1905	New Orleans	Yellow Fever (last U.S. outbreak)
1916	Nationwide	Polio (infantile paralysis)
1918	Worldwide	Influenza (more hospitalized in WWI from this epidemic than from battle; some U.S. Army training camps had 80% death rate)
1952	Nationwide	Polio
1962-65	Worldwide	Rubella (German measles)
1981-Present	Worldwide	HIV/AIDS

CHAPTER 2

Identifying

YOUR ANCESTORS

Before searching for that elusive ancestor ...

... you should have an idea and concept of relationship terms and definitions.

An *ancestor* is someone from whom you are directly descended. Parents, grandparents, great-grandparents and so on all fall into this category. Brothers, sisters, aunts, uncles and cousins do not fall into this category; these relatives are called collateral relationships. Although important to identify, they should not be labeled as ancestors.

It is also important to note the distinction between kith and kin. Kith are persons with whom you have a close relationship, not necessarily by blood. Today we might call these people our "chosen family." Close friends and mentors would fall into this category. Kin are blood relatives, the co-descendants of a common ancestor, whether patrilineal (father's side) or matrilineal (mother's side).

Descriptions of such relationships are often found on gravestones and other documents. "Beloved daughter of" and "wife of" and "husband of" are common carvings on gravestones. When reading these relationships, be very cautious. Misinterpreting or misunderstanding a relationship can send you looking in the wrong direction or leave you scratching your head.

Again, we cannot view gravestones – and even these relationship descriptions – with a 21st Century understanding. Ancestral distinctions – parents, grandparents and great-grandparents – as well as in-law labels share the same meaning as their modern definitions.

Other types of relationships can become more complicated. For example, the term "Mrs." did not necessarily mean the deceased was married. In times past, it could have simply implied a very high social status.

A person with any degree of relationship outside the immediate family was termed a "cousin." In early New England, it was even sometimes used to refer to a nephew or niece.

The word "nephew" comes from the Latin word *nepos*, meaning grandson. Occasionally, this usage will appear on old stones, where it can also mean grandchildren – male and female.

In the past, brothers and sisters-in-law were simply called "brother" and "sister" by a married couple. Some religious organizations also used the terms "brother" and "sister" to indicate membership in their respective group.

Modern usage of "Jr." and "Sr." implies a father-son relationship. But prior to the 19th Century, those terms could have also denoted an uncle, nephew or cousin relationship. It was not uncommon to find that those with the same surname – but not actually related by blood – often used those terms. Another thing to consider: when looking at old records, a "J.J. Jr." often becomes a "J.J. Sr." when the older man dies.

In short, social relationships can be complicated and confusing. It is best to check every available record you can find to make sure the relationship is being interpreted correctly.

Naming Procedure

Our ancestors often used the following naming procedure when picking out a name for a new child, which explains why certain names are extremely common in a given family line. Watching for these patterns can help in your research.

1st son – father's father

2nd son – mother's father

3rd son – father

4th son – father's oldest brother

5th son – father's second oldest brother or mother's oldest brother

1st daughter – mother's mother

2nd daughter – father's mother

3rd daughter – mother

4th daughter – mother's oldest sister

5th daughter – mother's second oldest sister or father's oldest sister

Surnames

Surnames should also be verified. When surnames were being adopted, many were the result of nicknames given by friends, relatives or others. Some of these were unflattering – to the point of vulgarity – but most of those have vanished, having been changed by descendants either by spelling or adopting a new name upon emigrating. Nicknames are perhaps the most fascinating surnames, but not always flattering to one's ancestors. Gotobed, for example, stemmed from someone who was lazy, while Kennedy is Gaelic for "ugly head."

Prominent physical features were often used as an identifier (Long, Short, Little, Beardsley, Stout), as were dispositions of the bearers (Gay, Moody, Stern, Wise). Sometimes the name told its own story (Lackland, Freeholder, Goodpasture, Upthegrove) and sometimes they might have even been selected to elicit envy or sympathy (Rich, Poor, Miracle, Armstrong).

Names that identify the father are termed patronymic surnames. (Rarely was the name of the mother used; in that case it is referred to as matronymic origin.) The Scandinavians added "son" to identify John's son or Erik's son. The Norman-French used the prefix "Fitz" to mean child of – as in Fitzpatrick, "child of Patrick." Many other cultures had their own prefixes to indicate the father's name, including the Scots (Macdonald), Irish (O'Brien), Dutch (Van Buren), French (de Gaulle), Germans (Von Berger), Spanish-Italian (D'Tello) and Arabs ('ibn-Saud). Sometimes the prefixes were attached to places, such as traditional family landholdings or estates, rather than the father's name.

Surnames based on the Christian name of the father are very common in English-speaking countries. Either the name is obvious (John William) or an "s" might be added, creating a name such as Williams. In some cases, the ending "son" is added so you get Davidson, Richardson, or Anderson (son of Andrew). Tennyson was the son of Dennis. Families which settled in Ireland following the Norman conquest have a surname beginning with "Fitz" (from the French "fils," for "son"). "Fitz", as used in England, can indicate illegitimacy.

The suffix "kin" can be used in surnames as a diminutive – so Tomkin is "Little Thomas," Wilkin is "Little William" and Perkin is "Little Peter." Similarly, Bartlett is Little Bartholomew, Dickens is the son of Little Dick and Philpott is Little Philip.

Indeed, a Christian name can be altered over time. The name David, for example, has become: Davey, Davids, Dowell, Davidson, Davidge, Davie, Davies, Daviess, Davis, Davison, Dayson, Davy, Davys, Daw, Dawe, Dawes, Dawkes, Dawkins, Daws, Dawson, Day, Davitt, Dowson, Dowd, Dowden and Dowling.

The baptismal name of Richard has been modified to give us: Dick, Dickens, Dickenson, Dickson, Dixon, Heacock, Hick, Hickin, Hickman, Hickmot, Hickox, Hicks, Hickson, Higgins, Higginson, Higgs, Higman, Hiscock, Hitch, Hitchcock, Hitchinson, Hitchmough, Hix, Reckett, Ricard, Rich, Richards, Riche, Richer, Richett, Richney, Richie, Richman, Rick, Rickard, Rickeard, Rickett, Ricketts, Rickman, Ricks, Rickson, Ritchie, Ritchard and Rix.

Welsh surnames can be difficult to trace since, though patronymic, they were not always hereditary. William's son Hugh, for example, was Hugh Williams. Hugh's son Richard was Richard Hughes and so on.

Some names were simply added when those without a surname suddenly needed one. A lady-in-waiting for royalty might have had no traditional surname, but would require one if no longer in the service of royalty. In times of political turmoil, a deposed ruler might require a smaller staff, and long-time servants would find themselves among commoners and suddenly in need of a surname. Names were sometimes invented as combinations of other words.

Among the most common names were taken from specialty crafts and trades. The Miller was essential for making flour from grain. The Sawyer cut timber into workable lengths, with which the Carpenter could make specialty items for villagers. Some names were a reflection of the place of employment rather than the job itself – the name Abbott generally refers to the man who was in the employ of the abbey as a servant or other worker. The man named Bishop more than likely worked at the house of the Bishop rather than holding the position. Some names were taken as titles that were originally less occupational, such as Mayor. Some surname occupations are no longer in existence, but were enough to identify a man in Medieval times.

Most occupational surnames are self-explanatory: Barber, Plumber, Baker, etc. However, other occupational surnames are not as obvious as they seem. A Farmer did not work in agriculture but collected taxes, and Banker is not an occupational surname at all, instead meaning "dweller on a hillside."

The most widely found category is that which contains surnames derived from a place easily recognizable when they were adopted. When a man left his homeland and moved to another country, he was distinguished from his neighbors by the identity of his homeland – Walsh hailed from Wales, Norman was from Normandy, Norris was Norwegian. Some men were from such renowned locales that the name of the city itself was the distinguishing reference, such as Paris. Towns were used in the same fashion, as were major rivers and geographic features.

Less obvious now are those names that identified a man by the location of his house. John Atwood lived at the woods, but exactly which one has long since been lost. Other names can be traced to the exact locale where the first to bear the name kept his residence. As with the patronymic designators, languages varied in the way a place was denoted, as in the Dutch name Van Gelder (from the county of Gelder). The Germans used Von as the French used de or De, and both often reflected aristocracy.

Surnames representing localities are easy to recognize if they come from a specific geographic area or part of land – Marsh, Middleton, Sidney or Ireland, for example. The evolution of language has made others much less obvious – Cullen ("back of the river") and Dunlop ("muddy hill").

While there are some individuals who strongly believe that all people with the same surname are related – based on the assumption that you only need go back far enough – this is in fact a major myth.

The reality is that surnames were not in use from the beginning of time, originating in Western culture only around 1300. Prior to that time they were hardly needed. A person had a given name and then some descriptive name based on occupation or locality. For instance, Daniel the cooper would eventually become Daniel Cooper. And, of course, a cooper was someone who made barrels.

It can be very interesting to delve into the origination of some surnames. For instance, Fallowell or Fallwell literally means "fall in the well." Yeager, a German surname, means "game hunter." The Norwegian surname Madsen means "son of the strong man." Szabo, a Hungarian surname, means "tailor."

Chinese surnames also have meanings. The surname Chieu means "to return to the original owner." Foong means "horse running." And the surname Chin means "to arrange or to exhibit."

It is important to remember that the spelling of these surnames often varies tremendously. For instance, the surname Lambert, which takes its name from "lamb herd" or "land bright," can have the following variations: Lambard, Lambart, Lambarth, Lambirth, Lamburd, Lampard, Lampart, Lamperd, Lampert, Lammert and Limbert. That's a lot of variants.

Sometimes researching the meaning behind a surname can be as much fun as researching family history. Whether you're a Waite (a watchman), a Yates (a gatekeeper) or an Osler (a birth catcher), continue to enjoy the search for your ancestors.

Family Crest or Coat of Arms

During the Middle Ages, knights and noblemen used padded linen, covered by metal and called a surcoat, to protect themselves from the heat. Charges, or base colors of the shield – along with colorful crests, shields and symbols – were displayed on these surcoats, which is where the term "coat of arms" comes from.

Since knights in armor looked similar to one another, their coat of arms was important in identifying them in battle, making it easier to distinguish between friend and foe.

The term hatchment, an old English word meaning attachment, refers to the entire coat of arms and its attachments, which can include the crest, mantling, coronet, helm, supporter, arms, motto scroll and compartment.

The main part of the coat of arms is the shield, which is often surrounded by various combinations of a crest, motto and supports, usually animals. Although the animals were usually shown in traditional postures, the depiction was not intended to be a realistic picture. Instead, they were drawn to illustrate the animal as a symbol. Usually fierce, sometimes even mythological, they were often shown in positions of combat.

The most common animals on shields include: a lion, bear, boar, eagle, horse, dragon, wolf, unicorn, hawk, raven and griffin. There are also names for the positions in which the animals are shown:

Rampant – standing on hind legs

Rampant guardant – standing on hind legs, facing the viewer

Passant – walking

Sejant – sitting

Couchant – lying down

The blazon is the description, or motto, of the shield, sometimes written in a vocabulary similar to Latin or old French.

The oldest son would often inherit his family's coat of arms without any changes. The younger brothers, however, would usually add symbols or pictures in the middle of the shield to identify themselves. When a woman married, her family's coat of arms was generally incorporated into that of her husband's. Many times, coats of arms were quartered or divided into different parts.

A common question among beginning researchers is whether their family might be entitled to use a coat of arms. Petitioning an organization like the College of Arms is one avenue toward this. Persons without a criminal record are rarely refused, provided that the coat of arms in question is historically correct. Other reputable companies simply search for the appropriate coat of arms using your surname, and are often able to provide a wide variety of products with the coat emblazoned on them.

Through the years, there has been much confusion regarding the term "family crest" versus the "coat of arms." The crest itself is a part of the coat of arms that appears above the shield. Gaelic tradition allowed family members to use the crest in a badge setting, resulting in it being displayed on engravings, rings, bookplates and other items for generations. Many authorities, however, claim that they were never intended to be used alone, without the remainder of the official coat of arms.

The most reliable research source is Fairbairn's *Book of Crests of the Families of Great Britain and Ireland*, which was first published in 1859 and has been revised and reprinted over the years.

Did Your Ancestor Fight in a War?

Born Between	War Possibly Involved In	Dates of War
1639-1743	Intercolonial Wars	1689-1765
1713-1740	Paxton Boys Uprising	1763-1764
1713-1743	Pontiac's Rebellion	1763-1765
1719-1755	Regulator War	1769-1771
1720-1763	American Revolution	1775-1783
1626-1656	Leisler's Rebellion	1776
1766-1787	Shays' Rebellion	1786-1787
1740-1791	Indian Wars	1790-1811
1744-1778	Whiskey Rebellion	1794
1762-1794	War of 1812	1812-1815
1762-1812	Black Hawk War	1832
1796-1828	Mexican War	1846-1848
1806-1850	Civil War	1861-1865
1848-1880	Spanish-American War	1898
1864-1900	World War I	1914-1918
1889-1929	World War II	1939 ('41 for US)-1945

Relationship Terms

AUGMENTED FAMILY   Extension of nuclear family to include people bound together by law, rather than blood; e.g. half siblings, adopted children, step-parents, step-siblings, etc.

AUNT   In American society, this term can refer to a woman in four different relative positions: father's sister, mother's sister, father's brother's wife, mother's brother's wife. Also used as a term of affection or respect, even without blood or legal relationship.

BROTHER   In addition to the obvious meaning, this term may also include: (1) the husband of one's sister; (2) the brother of one's wife; (3) the husband of one's sister-in-law; (4) half-brother; (5) step-brother. Genealogists must be aware that "brother" may also refer to a member of one's church.

COLLATERAL FAMILY   Referring to relatives who are "off to one side" (i.e., not in the direct lineal ancestry, but who share a common ancestor). In western society, they are called aunts, uncles, cousins, etc.

CONSANGUINITY   Refers to persons who share common descent or biological heritage.

COUSIN   Very general term in American society referring to someone with whom you share a common ancestor. Can refer to a person occupying relationship on either mother or father's side; may also refer to someone related only by affinity. If this person is in a different generation, the term "removed" is used giving the number of generations apart.

EXTENDED FAMILY   When families of more than two generations compose a household or relationship.

FULL SIBLING   One who has the same biological mother and father (thus the same ancestry) as oneself. A half-sibling has one of the same parents (and therefore shares only one side of the lineage) as oneself.

IN-LAW   In contemporary society, term used to designate someone to whom you are related by your own marriage or that of a sibling. In colonial society, this term also referred to relationships created by the marriage of a parent, currently called "step" relationships. Thus a "mother-in-law" in the 17th Century, may have been a father's second wife.

NATURAL CHILD   When the term "natural" is used, the researcher should not jump to a conclusion that it denotes an illegitimate relationship. It is meant to indicate a relationship by blood rather than one by marriage or adoption. An illegitimate child may be called "my base son" or "my bastard son."

NEPHEW/NIECE   One who is the child of a sibling (or a half-sibling, or step-sibling, or a spouse's sibling). Since the term derives from the Latin term "nepos," meaning grandson, it is possible an early colonial reference may have had this meaning.

"Now wife" Often assumed that the testator of a will using this term had a former wife. While this may be true, it is more likely the testator is indicating the bequest is intended only for his present wife and not necessarily to any subsequent wife he may have. Donald Lines Jacobus wrote, ".... it is to be doubted whether any other legal phrase has fooled so many of our most experienced genealogists."

Nuclear family A family group consisting of mother, father and dependent children.

"Once-removed" A relative referred to as once or more times removed represents a generational change. For example, your uncle or aunt's children are your first cousins. Your first cousins' children would be your first cousins once removed.

Step-sibling One related by virtue of a parent's marriage to an individual with children by a former marriage or relationship. While no relation by blood, there can be strong ties of emotion and tradition between step-siblings.

Uncle In American society, this term can refer to a man in four different relative positions: father's brother; mother's brother; father's sister's husband; mother's sister's husband. Also used as a term of affection or respect, even without blood or legal relationship.

Relationship Chart

Illustrating "Once Removed" ...

The relationship in each box is what that person's relationship would be to you, where you are "Self." You, your siblings, your first cousins, second cousins, etc., are all in the same generation. Thus, "once removed" means "one generation removed."

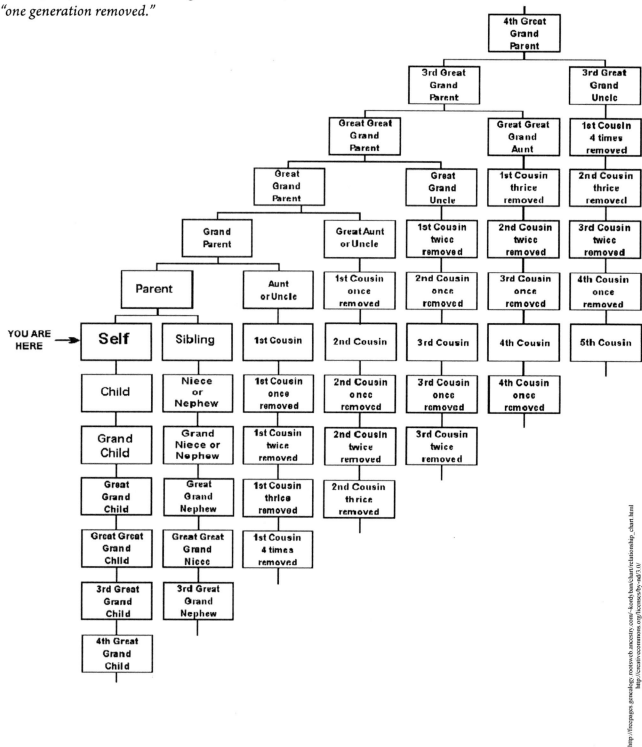

Pedigree Chart

Chart no. _____

No. 1 on this chart is the same as
no. _____ on pedigree chart no. _____

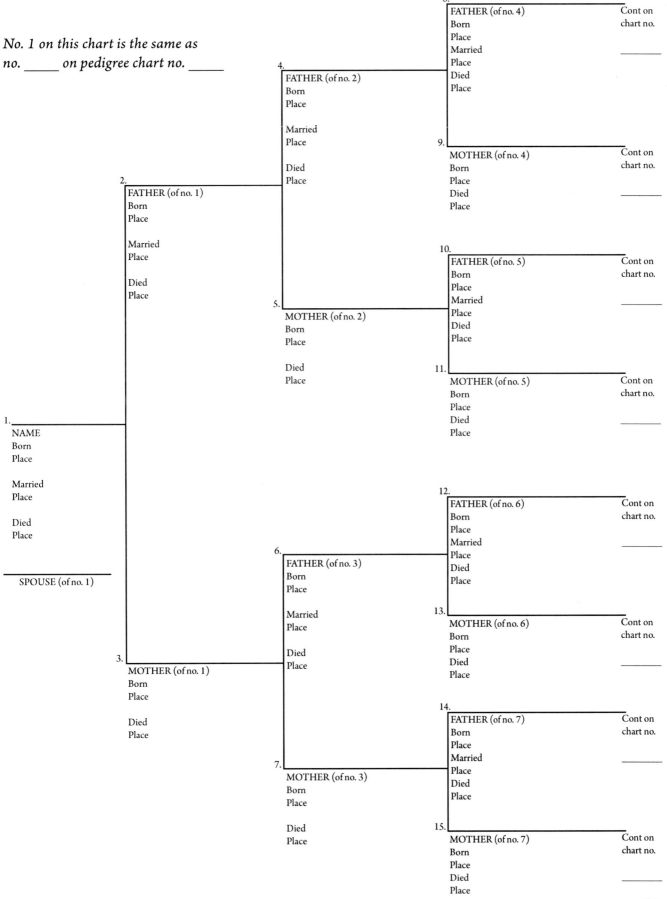

8. _____
FATHER (of no. 4)
Born
Place
Married
Place
Died
Place

Cont on
chart no.

_____

4. _____
FATHER (of no. 2)
Born
Place

Married
Place

Died
Place

9. _____
MOTHER (of no. 4)
Born
Place
Died
Place

Cont on
chart no.

_____

2. _____
FATHER (of no. 1)
Born
Place

Married
Place

Died
Place

10. _____
FATHER (of no. 5)
Born
Place
Married
Place
Died
Place

Cont on
chart no.

_____

5. _____
MOTHER (of no. 2)
Born
Place

Died
Place

11. _____
MOTHER (of no. 5)
Born
Place
Died
Place

Cont on
chart no.

_____

1. _____
NAME
Born
Place

Married
Place

Died
Place

_____
SPOUSE (of no. 1)

12. _____
FATHER (of no. 6)
Born
Place
Married
Place
Died
Place

Cont on
chart no.

_____

6. _____
FATHER (of no. 3)
Born
Place

Married
Place

Died
Place

13. _____
MOTHER (of no. 6)
Born
Place
Died
Place

Cont on
chart no.

_____

3. _____
MOTHER (of no. 1)
Born
Place

Died
Place

14. _____
FATHER (of no. 7)
Born
Place
Married
Place
Died
Place

Cont on
chart no.

_____

7. _____
MOTHER (of no. 3)
Born
Place

Died
Place

15. _____
MOTHER (of no. 7)
Born
Place
Died
Place

Cont on
chart no.

_____

35

Pedigree Chart Directions

Your Pedigree Chart becomes a map to the generations. Each person listed is a direct ancestor; therefore, you will want to follow both the male and female lines, as the charts connect.

On each chart, you can complete a line identifying a related chart: "Person #___ on this chart is the same as Person #____ on Chart #____." Next to the names of persons in the fourth generation of each chart, you can record the numbers of the continuation charts. Strive for consistency.

NAMES

1. Capitalize surnames; this makes them stand out.
2. For females, include maiden name (birth surname).
3. Add nicknames in quotation marks.
4. Use initials only when you don't know the full name; leave room to add the full name when you have acquired it.
5. Include middle names whenever they are known. Occasionally someone will have as many as four or even five names; your earliest ancestors may have had only one name.

DATES

6. Record dates as used in the military system. [Example: 4 July 1776]

PLACES

7. Record place names in this order separated by commas: city, county, state, country.
   [Example: Hiltons, Scott, VA, USA]
8. Use the accepted two-letter post office abbreviations for U.S. states. For contrast, use three letters for a country, which appears last.
9. Include the name and location of the cemetery burial place when known.

10. Use the Ahnentafel numbering system as you begin your research. This ingenious system allows researchers to properly display their ancestors in a compact manner without the need for a large-scale family tree. Other systems can be added later if desired. Most commercial genealogy database programs will use a unique numbering system but will often let you insert your own as well. Some software packages can even be instructed to run the Ahnentafel numbers and insert them for you.

    a. Number 1 may be male or female. (YOU)

    b. All even numbers thereafter are MALE.

    c. All odd numbers from 3 on are FEMALE.

    d. To find the father of a person, double that person's number.

    e. To find the mother of a person, double that person's number and add one. The wife is always one number higher than her husband is.

*Family Group Sheet*

_____ *on this chart is the same as*
no. _____ *on pedigree chart no.* _____

HUSBAND _____ IdentificationNumber _____
Birth Date _____ Place _____
Christening Date _____ Place _____
Marriage Date _____ Place _____
Death Date _____ Place _____
Burial Date _____ Place _____
Father of Husband _____ MotherofHusband _____

WIFE _____ IdentificationNumber _____
Birth Date _____ Place _____
Christening Date _____ Place _____
Marriage Date _____ Place _____
Death Date _____ Place _____
Burial Date _____ Place _____
Father of Wife _____ MotherofWife _____

CHILDREN *(check box next to name of direct-line ancestor)*
#1 ☐ Name _____ Identification Number _____
Birth Date _____ Place _____
Christening Date _____ Place _____
Death Date _____ Place _____
Burial Date _____ Place _____
Marriage Date _____ MarriedWhom _____

#2 ☐ Name _____ Identification Number _____
Birth Date _____ Place _____
Christening Date _____ Place _____
Death Date _____ Place _____
Burial Date _____ Place _____
Marriage Date _____ MarriedWhom _____

#3 ☐ Name _____ Identification Number _____
Birth Date _____ Place _____
Christening Date _____ Place _____
Death Date _____ Place _____
Burial Date _____ Place _____
Marriage Date _____ MarriedWhom _____

#4 ☐ Name _____ Identification Number _____
Birth Date _____ Place _____
Christening Date _____ Place _____
Death Date _____ Place _____
Burial Date _____ Place _____
Marriage Date _____ MarriedWhom _____

Family Group Sheet Directions

Completed family records will provide the following information: name of husband with the date and place of his birth, marriage, death, burial, and the names of his parents, as well as an Ahnentafel identification number. Wife's and childrens' records should be formatted in the same fashion. Most forms offer space also to insert information such as occupation, church affiliation, military service and perhaps places of residence.

The advantage of a Family Group Sheet over a Pedigree Chart is that it gives you more information about the parents and provides the names of all the children, together with their spouses. As you continue searching for your direct ancestors, you often will find your leads by way of these "collateral" lines. You may have difficulty locating your own ancestor, but his brother or brother-in-law may have appeared in more written records and provide helpful clues as a result. Strive for consistency.

1. For each marriage on your Pedigree Chart, fill out a Family Group Sheet.

2. Follow the same rules as for the Pedigree Chart with regard to names, dates and places.

3. The father's vital information should appear at the top of the page and should also include his identification number. The names of his parents should also appear here.

4. The wife's vital information follows that of the husband. List her parents' names also.

5. Next comes a listing of the children, in order of birth when known and with indication whether male or female. It isn't necessary to include the surname unless the individual took a different spelling; even this would ordinarily appear on the family group record where he/she is a part of a parental couple. However, on a computerized record, because linkage is automatic, you may need to record the surname the first time you enter the individual.

6. Include only one family unit on this sheet. If there is a second marriage recorded on a separate sheet, the name of another spouse should also appear on this chart to remind you that there is another marriage and possibly other children.

7. Use the backside of the sheet to make notes and to document the sources of your information.

Glossary of Genealogy-Related Terms

Abstract - Summary of important points of a given text, especially deeds and wills

Acre - See *Measurements*

Administration (estate) - Collection, management, distribution of an estate by proper legal process

Administrator (estate) - Person appointed to manage or divide the estate of a deceased person

Administratrix - A female administrator

Affidavit - A statement in writing, sworn to before proper authority

Alien - Foreigner

American Revolution - U.S. war for independence from Great Britain, 1775 -1783

Ancestor - A person from whom you are descended; a forefather or foremother

Ante - Latin prefix meaning *before*, as in "antebellum South" (the South before the war)

Apprentice - One who is bound by indentures, by legal agreement or by any means to serve another person for a certain time, with a view of learning an art or trade

Appurtenance - Something belonging to/with something else (i.e., a building, orchard, right of way)

Archives - Records of a government, organization, institution; the place where records are stored

Attest - To affirm; to certify by signature or oath

Banns - Public announcement of intended marriage

Beneficiary - One who receives benefit of trust or property

Bequeath - To give personal property to a person in a will

Bond - Written, signed, witnessed agreement requiring payment of a specified amount of money on or before a given date

Bounty Land Warrant - A right to obtain land; specific number of acres of unallocated public land granted for military service

Census - Official enumeration, listing or counting of citizens

Certified Copy - A copy made and attested to by officers having charge of the original and authorized to give copies

Chain - See *Measurements*

Chattel - Personal property that can include animate as well as inanimate properties

Christen - To receive or initiate into the visible church by baptism; to name at baptism; to give a name

Circa - About, near, or approximate; usually referring to a date

Civil War - War Between The States; war between North and South, 1861-65

Codicil - Addition to a will

Collateral Ancestor - Belong to the same ancestral stock but not in direct line of descent; opposed to lineal such as aunts, uncles & cousins.

Common Ancestor - Ancestor shared by any two people

Confederate - In history, pertains to the southern states (as well as their governments and citizens) that seceded from the Union in 1860 -1861, an act that brought about the U.S. Civil War

Consanguinity - Blood relationship

Consort - Usually a wife whose husband is living; a companion

Conveyance - See *Deed*

Cousin - Relative descended from a common ancestor, but not a brother or sister

Deceased - Dead

Decedent - A deceased person

Declaration of Intention - Paper sworn to and filed in court by an alien stating desire for citizenship

Deed - A document of conveyance by which title in real property is transferred from one party to another

Deposition - A testifying or testimony taken down in writing under oath of affirmation in reply to interrogatories, before a competent officer to replace the oral testimony of a witness

Devise - Gift of real property by will

Devisee - One to whom real property is given in a will

Devisor - One who gives real property in a will

Dissenter - One who did not belong to the established church, such as someone who opposed the Church of England in the American colonies

District Land Office Plat Book - Books or maps that show the location of the land patentee

District Land Office Tract Book - Books that list individual entries by range and township

Double Dating - A system of double dating used in England and America from 1582-1752 because it was not clear as to whether the year commenced January 1 or March 25

Dower - Legal right or share which a wife acquired by marriage in the real estate of her husband, allotted to her after his death for her lifetime

Emigrant - A person who leaves one country to move to another

Enumeration - Listing or counting, such as for a census

Epitaph - An inscription on or at a tomb or grave in memory of the one buried there

Escheat - The reversion of property to the state when there are no qualified heirs

Estate - All property and debts belonging to a person

Et Al - Latin for "and others"

Et Uxor - Latin for "and wife"; sometimes written simply **Et Ux**

Executor - A man appointed in a will to carry out its provisions

Executrix - A woman appointed in a will to carry out its provisions

Fee - An estate of inheritance in land, being either fee simple or fee tail; an estate in land held of a feudal lord on condition of the performing of certain services

Fee Simple - An absolute ownership without restriction

Fee Tail - An estate of inheritance limited to lineal descendant heirs of a person to whom it was granted

Franklin, State of - An area once known but never officially recognized and was under consideration from 1784 - 1788 from the western part of North Carolina

Fraternity - Group of men or women sharing a common purpose or interest

Free Hold - An estate in fee simple, in fee tail, or for life

Friend - Member of the religious Society of Friends; a Quaker

Furlong - See *Measurements*

Gazetteer - Geographical dictionary with place names and descriptions, usually in alphabetical order

Genealogy - Study of family history and descent

Gentleman - A man well-born

Given Name - Name given to a person at birth or baptism; one's first and middle names

Glebe - Land belonging to a parish church

Grantee - One who buys property or receives a grant

Grantor - One who sells property or makes a grant

Guardian - Person appointed to care for and manage property of a minor orphan or an adult incompetent of managing his own affairs

Heirs - Those entitled by law or by the terms of a will to inherit property from another

Holographic Will - One written entirely in the testator's own handwriting

Homestead Act - Law passed by Congress in 1862 allowing a head of a family to obtain title to 160 acres of public land after clearing and improving it for five years

Hugenot - A French Protestant in the 16th and 17th centuries; one of the Reformed or Calvinistic communion who were driven by the thousands into exile in England, Holland, Germany and America

Illegitimate - Born to a mother who was not married to the child's father; bastard

Immigrant - A person who moves into one country from another

Indenture - Today it means a contract in two or more copies; originally made in two parts by cutting or tearing a single sheet across the middle in a jagged line so the parts might later be matched

Indentured Servant - One who bound himself into service of another person for a specified number of years, often in return for transportation to a new country

Infant - Any person not of full age; a minor

Instant - Of or pertaining to the current month

Intestate - One who dies without a will or dying without a will

Inventory - An account, catalog or schedule, made by an executor or administrator of all the goods and chattels and, sometimes, real estate of a deceased person

Issue - Offspring; children; lineal descendants of a common ancestor

Late - Recently deceased

Lease - An agreement between a landlord and tenant

Legacy - Property or money left to someone in a will

Legislature - Lawmaking branch of state or national government; elected group of lawmakers

Lien - A claim against property as security for payment of a debt

Lineage - Ancestry; direct descent from a specific ancestor

Lineal - Consisting of or being in a direct line of ancestry or descendants; descended in a direct line

Link - See *Measurements*

Lis Pendens - Pending court action; usually applies to land title claims

Lodge - A chapter or meeting hall of a fraternal organization

Loyalist - Tory; an American colonist who supported the British side during the American Revolution

Maiden Name - Birth name; a girl's family surname; a woman's surname before she marries

Manuscript - Narative or music written with the hand or typeset in unpublished draft form

Marriage Bond - A financial guarantee that no impediment to the marriage existed, furnished by the intended bridegroom or by his friends

Maternal / Matrilineal - Lineage through one's mother

Measurements -

    Link - 7.92 inches

    Chain - 100 links or 66 feet

    Furlong - 1000 links or 660 feet

    Rod - 5 1/2 yards or 16 1/2 feet (also called a **Perch** or **Pole**)

    Rood - from 5 1/2 yards to 8 yards, depending on locality

    Acre - 43,560 square feet or 160 square rods

Messuage - A dwelling house

Metes & Bounds - Property described by natural boundaries, such as "three notches in a white oak tree"

Microfiche - Sheet of microfilm with greatly reduced images of pages of documents

Microfilm - Reproduction of documents on film at reduced size

Migrant - Person who moves from place to place, usually in search of work

Migrate - To move from one country or state or region to another

Militia - Citizens of a state who are not part of the national military forces but who can be called into military service in an emergency; a citizen army, apart from the regular military forces

Minor - One who is under legal age; not yet a legal adult

Mister - In early times, a title of respect given only to those who held important civil offices or who were of "gentle" blood

Moiety - A half; an indefinite portion

Mortality - Death; death rate

Mortality Schedules - Enumeration of persons who died during the year prior to June 1 of 1850, 1860, 1870 and 1880 in each state of the United States, conducted by the Bureau of the Census

Mortgage - A conditional transfer of title to real property as security for payment of a debt

Namesake - Person named after another person

Necrology - Listing or record of persons who have died recently; obituary

Nee - Used to identify a woman's maiden name; means "born with the surname of"

Noncupative Will - One declared or dictated by the testator, usually for persons in last sickness, sudden illness, or military

Orphan - Child whose parents are dead; sometimes, a child who has lost one parent by death

Orphan's Court - Orphans being recognized as wards of the state; historically, provisions were made for them in special courts

Passenger List - A ship's list (manifest) of passengers, usually referring to those ships arriving in the U.S. or Canada from Europe

Patent - Grant of land from a government to an individual

Paternal / Patrilineal - Lineage through one's father

Patriot - One who has emotional attachment to her/his country and supports its interests

Pedigree - Family tree; ancestry

Pension - Money paid regularly to an individual, especially by a government as reward for military service during wartime or upon retirement from government service

Pensioner - One who receives a pension

Perch - See *Measurements*

Pole - See *Measurements*

Poll - List or record of persons, especially for taxing or voting

Post - Prefix meaning *after*, as in "post-war economy"

Posterity - Descendants; those who come after

Power of Attorney - When a person is unable to act for himself, he appoints another to act in his behalf

Pre - Prefix meaning *before*, as in "pre-war buildup"

Pre-emotion Rights - Right given by the federal government to citizens to buy a quarter section, or less, of land

Probate - Having to do with wills and the administration of estates

Progenitor - A direct ancestor

Progeny - Descendants of a common ancestor; issue

Proved Will - A will established as genuine by probate court

Provost - A person appointed to superintend or preside over something

Proximo - In the following month, in the month after the present

Public Domain - Land owned by the government

Quaker - Member of the religious Society of Friends

Quitclaim - A deed conveying the interest of the party at that time

Rector - A clergyman; the ruler or governor of a country

Relict - Widow or widower; surviving spouse when husband or wife has died

Republic - Government in which supreme authority lies with the people or their elected representatives

Revolutionary War - U.S. war for independence from Great Britain, 1775 -1783

Rod - See *Measurements*

Rood - See *Measurements*

Shaker - Member of a religious group formed in 1747 that practiced communal living and celibacy

Sic - Latin meaning *thus*; copied exactly as the original reads; suggests a mistake or surprise in original

Spinster - An unmarried woman; one who spins

Sponsor - A bondsman; surety

Statute - Law

Surname - Family name or last name

Territory - Area of land owned by a country, not a state or province, but having its own legislature and governor

Testamentary - Pertaining to a will

Testate - A person who dies leaving a valid will

Testator - A person who makes a valid will before his death

Tithable - Taxable

Tithe - Historically, money due as a tax for support of the clergy or church

Tory - Loyalist; a colonist who supported the British side in the American Revolution

Township - A division of U.S. public land that contained thirty-six sections of square miles; in some locales, a subdivision of a county; a small town or village

Tradition - The handing down of statements, beliefs, legends, customs, genealogies, etc., from generation to generation, especially by word of mouth (as in "the oral tradition")

Transcribe - To make a copy in writing

Ultimo - In the month before this one

Union - The United States; also the North during the U.S. Civil War; the states that did not secede

Verbatim - Word for word; in the same words

Vital Records - Records of birth, death, marriage or divorce

Vital Statistics - Data dealing with birth, death, marriage or divorce

War Between The States - U.S. Civil War, 1861-1865

Ward - Chiefly the division of a city or county for election purposes

Will - Document declaring how a person wants property divided after her/his death

Witness - One who is present at a transaction, such as a sale of land or signing of a will, who can testify or affirm that it actually took place

WPA Historical Records Survey - A program undertaken by the U.S. government from 1935-1936 in which inventories were compiled of historical material

Accomptant - Accountant

Almoner - Giver of charity to the needy

Amanuensis - Secretary or stenographer

Artificer - A soldier mechanic who does repairs

Bailie - Bailiff

Baxter - Baker

Blacksmith - One who shoes horses

Bluestocking - Female intellectual and writer

Boniface - Keeper of an inn

Brazier - One who works with brass

Brewster - Beer manufacturer

Brightsmith - Metal worker

Burgonmaster - Mayor

Caulker - One who fills up cracks in ships, around windows, or along seams to make them watertight by using tar and/or oakum-hemp fiber acquired by unravelling old ropes

Chaisemaker - Carriage maker

Chandler - Dealer or trader; one who makes or sells candles; retailer of groceries

Chiffonnier - Wig maker

Clark - Clerk

Clerk - Clergyman, cleric

Clicker - The servant of a salesman who stands at the door to invite customers; one who receives type in galleys from the compositors to arrange it for printing; one who makes eyelet holes in boots using a machine which clicks

Cobbler - One who makes or repairs shoes and boots

Cohen - Priest; descendant of Levi

Collier - Coal miner

Colporteur - Peddler of books

Cooper - One who makes or repairs vessels made of staves and hoops (casks, barrels, tubs, etc.)

Cordwainer - Shoemaker, originally any leather worker using leather from Cordova (Cordoba) in Spain

Costermonger - Peddler of fruits and vegetables

Crocker - Potter

Crowner - Coroner

Currier - One who dresses the coat of a horse with a currycomb; one who tans leather by incorporating oil or grease

Docker / Stevedore - Dock worker who loads and unloads cargo

Dowser - One who finds water using a rod or "witching stick"

Draper - A dealer in dry goods

Drayman - One who drives a long, strong cart without fixed sides for carrying heavy loads

Dresser - A surgeon's assistant in a hospital

Drover - One who drives cattle, sheep, etc., to market; a dealer in cattle

Duffer - Peddler

Factor - Agent; commission merchant; one who acts or transacts business for another; Scottish steward or bailiff of an estate farrier

Faulkner - Falconer

Fell monger - One who removes hair or wool from hides in preparation for leather making

Fletcher - One who makes arrows by attaching feathers for sustained and accurate flight

Fuller - One who "fulls" cloth, then shrinks and thickens woolen cloth by moistening, heating, and pressing; a cloth cleaning and finishing worker

Gaoler - A keeper of the jail (gaol); a jailer

Glazier - Window glassman

Hacker - Maker of hoes

Hatcheler - One who combs out or cards flax

Haymonger - Dealer in hay

Hayward - Keeper of fences

Higgler - Itinerant peddler

Hillier - Roof tiler

Hind - Farm laborer

Hostler - Groom who takes care of horses, often at an inn

Hooker - Reaper

Hooper - One who makes hoops for casks and barrels

Huckster - Seller of small wares

Husbandman - Farmer who cultivates the land

Jagger - Fish peddler

Journeyman - One who has served an apprenticeship and mastered a craft; not bound to serve a master, but hired by the day

Joyner / Joiner - Skilled carpenter

Keeler - Bargeman

Kempster - Wool comber

Lardner - Keeper of the cupboard

Lavender - Washer woman

Lederer - Leather maker

Leech - Physician

Lormer - Maker of horse gear

Malender - Farmer

Maltster - Brewer

Manciple - A steward

Mason - Bricklayer

Mintmaster - One who issues local currency

Monger - Seller of goods (ale, fish, etc.)

Muleskinner - Teamster

Neatherder - Herder of cows

Ordinary Keeper - Innkeeper with fixed prices

Pattern Maker - Maker of a clog shod with an iron ring (a clog was a wooden pole with a pattern cut into the end)

Peregrinator - Itinerant wanderer

Peruker - A wig maker

Pettifogger - A shyster lawyer

Pigman - Crockery dealer

Plumber - One who applies sheet lead for roofing and lead frames for plain or stained glass windows

Porter - Doorkeeper

Puddler - Wrought iron worker

Quarrier - Quarry worker

Rigger - Hoist tackle worker

Ripper - Seller of fish

Roper - Maker of rope or nets

Saddler - One who makes, repairs or sells saddles or other furnishings for horses

Sawbones - Physician

Sawyer - One who saws; carpenter

Schumacker - Shoemaker

Scribbler - Person who writes for a living

Scrivener - Professional writer; scribe; public copyist; notary public

Scrutiner - Election judge

Shrieve - Sheriff

Slater - Roofer

Slopseller - Seller of ready-made clothes in a "slop shop"

Snobscat/Snob - One who repairs shoes

Sorter - Tailor

Spinster - A woman who spins; an unmarried woman

Spurrier - Maker of spurs

Squire - Country gentleman; farm owner; justice of peace

Stevedor - longshoreman

Stuff gown / Stuff gownsman - Junior barrister

Supercargo - Officer on merchant ship who is in charge of cargo and commercial concerns

Tanner - One who tans animal hides into leather

Tapley - One who puts the tap in an ale cask

Tasker - Reaper

Teamster - One who drives a team for hauling

Thatcher - Roofer

Tide waiter - Customs inspector

Tinker - An itinerant tin pot and pan seller and repairer

Tipstaff - Policeman

Travers - Toll bridge collector

Tucker - Cleaner of cloth goods

Turner - A person who turns wood on a lathe into spindles

Victualer - Tavern keeper; one who provides an army, navy, or ship with food

Vulcan - Blacksmith

Wagoner - Teamster not for hire

Wainwright - Wagon maker

Waiter - Customs officer or tide waiter; one who waits on the tide to collect duty on goods brought in

Waterman - Boatman who plies for hire

Webster - Operator of looms

Wharfinger - Owner of a wharf

Wheelwright - One who makes or repairs wheels, wheeled carriages, etc.

Whitesmith - Tinsmith; worker of iron who finishes or polishes the work

Whitewing - Street sweeper

Whitster - Bleacher of cloth

Wright - Workman; skilled worker

Yeoman - Farmer who owns his own land; servant, attendant or subordinate official in a royal
or affluent household.

CHAPTER 3

Finding a
CEMETERY

Locating graves of ancestors is often easy.

It's first finding the cemetery they're buried in that can be complicated and frustrating.

Names change over time. Local place names may not be the ones officially recorded; cartographers and record-keepers typically use official names, while many of small communities are known in their regional vernacular.

The graves of ancestors who died during and after the late 19th Century are generally easy to locate. Home sources, such as funeral cards and oral histories, can be very helpful. Death certificates and obituaries traditionally carry this information as well. Funeral homes are often good resources. The American Blue Book of Funeral Directors or similar directories are available in the reference section of many public libraries. If a funeral home no longer exists, contact the local or state historical society or local public library to ask if they know what happened to the records. For the curious with extra money, there is always the option of hiring a professional genealogist to track down the cemetery and grave of an ancestor, often using Global Positioning Satellite (GPS) coordinates.

Finding the graves of ancestors who passed away before the late 1800s may require more creativity. Knowing the locality where the ancestor died is helpful; chances are good that it's where they are buried.

Many individuals and organizations have transcribed the graves in cemeteries, publishing their findings. Visiting the Family History Library online at **www.familysearch.org** can also be helpful. The online catalog has perhaps the largest collection of published cemetery transcriptions currently available.

Other cemetery and tombstone registries are appearing online and across the country. The popular website **www.usgenweb.com** has its own location program where volunteers transcribe cemeteries and post them on the Internet.

In addition, a cemetery project hosted by the Kentucky Historical Society has attempted to map all the graves in the Commonwealth. Public libraries across Kentucky have copies of these maps indexed by cemetery and by person. Other states are following suit.

Types of Cemeteries

Technically speaking, a *graveyard* is connected to a church, while a *cemetery* may not be. However, these two terms have come to be used synonymously over the years; they are, in fact, used as synonyms in this book. There are *nine* basic types of cemeteries in the United States:

1. **THE CHURCH CEMETERY.** This cemetery may be adjacent to a church, in which case it may be known as a graveyard or "churchyard." Alternatively, it may be separate from the church. The cemetery is owned by the church and is private property, though normally it is open to all. Burial costs typically are low to moderate in this type of cemetery.

2. **THE PUBLIC CEMETERY.** This cemetery is owned by a governmental unit, usually a town, city, or county. By law, public cemeteries must be open to the public, although there may be limitations designed to discourage abusers. Burial costs typically are low in public cemeteries.

3. **THE CUSTOMARY CEMETERY.** This type of cemetery is simply a plot used by neighbors as a burying place. It has no formal or legal status, so there is no sexton (nor sexton's records), unless an individual decided to keep records as a public service. Customary cemeteries usually are cared for by the survivors of those buried within; sometimes they are scarcely cared for at all. Customary cemeteries are most common in rural areas. Often they are not legal, but they usually are tolerated well. Customary cemeteries have few or no burial costs.

4. **THE PRIVATE CEMETERY.** This type of cemetery is owned by a corporation and (in most states) must post information to that effect at the gate. It is run as a for-profit corporation and often has quite restrictive rules for markers and offerings, rules that usually are designed to cut maintenance costs. Burial costs at private cemeteries usually run from moderate to high.

5. THE LODGE CEMETERY. These cemeteries are owned and operated by lodges or other fraternal organizations, especially the Masons or Odd Fellows. These cemeteries sometimes are restricted to members of the organization, but often others can purchase plots. Many of these organizations were founded in part to provide burial insurance, and they often were inexpensive for members.

6. THE ETHNIC CEMETERY. To a certain extent, this category overlaps with some of the others, since an ethnic group may also be a religious group (*e.g.,* Russians and the Russian Orthodox Church). An ethnic cemetery can be public (*e.g.,* one owned by a Native American tribe), private, or customary. This category is especially useful for cemeteries that otherwise would be difficult to classify.

7. THE FAMILY CEMETERY. This type of cemetery remains legal in most states, and at one time there were many thousands of them in the United States. This is a plot of land, owned by a family and given over to the burial of its family members. Close friends are occasionally included.

8. THE MASS GRAVE. The victims of disasters sometimes are buried in a common grave. Often a memorial is erected to their memory afterward. The Earthquake Cemetery in Lone Pine, California, for example, is the mass grave of the victims of a major earthquake in 1872.

9. THE MILITARY CEMETERY. Where veterans can be granted a burial plot and a headstone at government expense.

Getting the Most out of Your Visit

History abounds in cemeteries. Acute observation with the eye of a detective will yield evidence – the names of people buried there, their familial relationships, their religious beliefs, their social standings, their technological knowledge, their cultural symbols and their artistic ideals. Here are some things to consider *in preparation* for your visit to a cemetery that will be useful to your research:

- **GET PERMISSION TO GO ON PRIVATE LAND.**
- **OBSERVE WITHOUT ALTERING.**
- **MAKE PHOTOGRAPHS, SKETCHES AND NOTES.**
- **LEAVE EVERYTHING EXACTLY AS YOU FOUND IT.**

These are good practices to observe *during* your visit:

- **BRING MATERIALS TO MAKE A RECORD OF WHAT YOU FIND.** This includes pencil, paper, camera and clipboard.
- **MAKE A MAP OF THE CEMETERY IF YOU NEED TO RECORD PARTICULAR DATA AND ITS PLACEMENT.** Use graph paper or draw a grid to scale. Letter an axis along the bottom, one letter to a square, and number a vertical axis along the left-hand side, one number to a square. This will

make each square identifiable by a unique number-letter combination. Make a corresponding grid on the site using string laid out in squares. Draw or refer to information according to the grid squares where something relevant is found. For instance, if you are studying the design of gravestones, you will want to include measurements of each stone, photos, rubbings, sketches of engravings, and notes about dating.

- **LOOK AT THE GRAVEYARD'S SURROUNDINGS.** Observe where it is located in relation to the landscape as a whole. Is it on a hilltop by itself, looking out across an expanse of mountains? Is it tucked away in a beautiful spot? Is it on land that is considered valuable, such as in a choice spot with good soil, or is it considered expendable? How would the natural landscape have looked at the time of burial, and how does that differ from how the site looks today? What conclusions can be drawn about the relationship of the graveyard to the landscape as a whole?

- **OBSERVE WHERE THE CEMETERY IS LOCATED IN RELATION TO OTHER HUMANMADE SPACES.** Is it next to a meetinghouse and limited to people of that religion? Is it secluded? Is it by a frequently traveled roadway? Can it be seen from the house where the deceased's family lived? Is there a division between holy ground and unholy ground? How would the humanmade landscape have looked at the time of burial, and how does that differ from how the site looks today? What conclusions can be drawn about the relationship of the graveyard to the rest of the humanmade landscape?

- **ANALYZE THE GEOGRAPHY.** Observe how the cemetery is defined as a space. What kinds of walls or fences are there, and what materials were used to make them? Are they fancy or plain, made of local or imported materials, of crude or of fine craftsmanship? What kinds of gates are there, and what materials were used to build them? Is there any apparent distinction between the sacred graveyard and space used for everyday activities? Is the land public or private? Is this the graveyard of a family, neighborhood, religious sect or community?

- **SEE IF DIFFERENT PARTS OF THE GRAVEYARD ARE USED FOR DIFFERENT PURPOSES.** Are there roadways between sections with ruts made by horse-drawn vehicles? Is there a tomb for use in the winter when the ground is frozen? What marks boundaries between sections?

- **OBSERVE THE OVERALL DESIGN OF THE SPACE.** Are there paths? What is their layout? Is there seating? An area for contemplation? Are there artificially created features such as promontories

and ponds? What does one see from different spots on the site? What is the overall intention? Stop for a moment and be quiet – what is the feeling of the place?

- **LOOK AT THE PLANTINGS.** Identify the flowers, herbs, shrubs, and trees. Even in an overgrown graveyard, some of the landscaping might still survive around the gate. Which plants are native and which have been imported? Which were planted and which are volunteers? Which are characteristic of practices during particular time periods? For instance, during the 19th Century, exotics such as wisteria were popular. Do the plants have symbolism? Mulberries were associated with the silkworm, for example, which was associated with the image of resurrection.

- **FOCUS ON THE MARKERS.** Observe the dates on the markers. What is the range of dates represented? How do these dates compare with the dates of other humanmade structures in the surrounding area? What conclusions can be drawn about its beginning and periods of active use? Did a group of people die around the same time, perhaps indicating an epidemic or disaster? Were these people of similar or different ages? What did they have in common?

- **OBSERVE THE GENERAL ARRANGEMENT OF MARKERS.** What kinds of people merited large markers and what kinds received medium and small markers? Is there a section with higher or more elaborate stones where the more prominent people are buried? Are there sections with no markers, where paupers or servants might have been buried with wooden markers that have rotted away? Are markers arranged in family clusters, perhaps several smaller ones around a larger marker enclosed by curbing? Is there a east-west orientation to the cemetery, reflecting the Christian belief that when the body sits up at the sunrise of resurrection, it will face east?

- **OBSERVE THE TYPES OF MARKERS USED.** Of what are the markers made? Are the markers of local or imported materials? Are they simple, ornamental, crude, finely worked? Do designs and materials vary according to the status of the person buried there? Do designs and materials vary according to the dates of burials?

- **CONSIDER HOW CHANGES IN MARKERS REFLECT CHANGES IN TECHNOLOGY.** What tools were used to make the markers? Were they made by hand or by machine? Were they factory-produced? Are materials used in the markers humanmade? For instance, in the late 19th Century, there were cast aluminum markers. By end of the 20th Century, a revival of contemporary art or personal imagery began, even with photographs of the deceased etched into stone or transferred onto metal.

- **OBSERVE THE DESIGNS OF THE MARKERS AND THEIR WRITING.** What shapes are used? What symbols are used and what are their meanings? What styles of lettering are used? What decorative elements are used? How do all of these vary with time? Do any of these seem to follow particular styles tied to particular periods?

- **GATHER EVIDENCE ABOUT THE PEOPLE BURIED HERE.** Determine the languages of the individual markers. In what languages are the markers written? What conclusions can you draw?

- **TRY TO FIGURE OUT THE ETHNICITIES OF THE DECEASED.** Use the language, names, and design elements as hints. Are certain dates and time periods associated with particular ethnicities? Do these dates represent the arrival or departure of certain groups from the area?

- **OBSERVE THE EPITAPHS.** Are there few or many words? Usually carvers charge by the letter. Do the markers of prominent people have more writing? What is the content of the epitaphs? What are the sources of verses or quotations? What beliefs about life or death do the epitaphs indicate? What do the epitaphs say about the lives of the deceased?

- **LOOK FOR SPECIAL MARKERS INDICATING MILITARY SERVICE OR GROUP MEMBERSHIPS.** To what military branch did people belong? In what wars did people fight? To what fraternal organizations (e.g., Odd Fellows, Masons, Elks, Woodmen) did they belong?

- **GATHER GENEALOGICAL INFORMATION FROM THE MARKERS.** At least some information such as date of birth and date of death can usually be found. Family relationships and status in life are also frequently indicated on gravestones.

- **OBSERVE WHO IS BURIED WITH WHOM.** Who is buried near whom and who is buried far away? (In some graveyards, for instance, women are buried with their mothers rather than their husbands.) Who is buried with their in-laws? Are slaves and servants buried near their masters? Where are children buried? What does this say about social and family ties in the era? Are there any animals buried here? What is the significance of their presence and placement?

- **LOOK FOR GRAVES JUST OUTSIDE THE MAIN ENCLOSURE.** The remains of slaves, suicides, or people professing a different religion from the majority were sometimes buried outside the main graveyard. How do these graves compare with graves inside the enclosure?

- **OBSERVE EVIDENCE OF MOURNING RITUALS.** What objects are left at the graves – flowers, toys for children, food? Are the graves well-kept? Who tends the graves? Are there people visiting the site? What are they doing?

- **SEARCH FOR SUPPORTING DOCUMENTATION.** Find documents that can verify what you have found or give you more information. Most cemeteries now have records of who is buried and where. These might be found at the town clerk's or in the graveyard office. Detailed information might be found in the register of deeds and probates, in church records, or in clerics' records. Private diaries and letters or family papers might yield information about private family plots. Town histories give information about people and times that can be linked to those buried.

- **PUT IT TOGETHER.** Make good notes or copies of what you find while you are on site. You might not be able to return later for more information. Write a summary of your findings and conclusions based on the entire body of evidence. Some conclusions may be possible only in light of all the evidence. Likewise, a single discovery can cause you to rethink your previous conclusions. Use your imagination and see what links you can make in this puzzle!

- **SHARE WHAT YOU FIND WITH OTHERS INTERESTED IN THE SUBJECTS OF YOUR SEARCH.** You may help them, they may help you, and you will trade ideas.

- **ORGANIZE YOUR DOCUMENTS, NOTES AND CONCLUSIONS.** Copy them so you have a second set. Archive them. Store the sets in two different, safe places.

Much documentation can be achieved with photography. Photographs are a wonderful way to document graveyards, both from scenic views of the cemetery to the inscriptions of individual tombstones. Digital cameras are relatively cheap and reliable. Even if you do not own a computer, the camera card can be used to print pictures at practically any photo outlet.

It is not every day that you get to visit an ancestor's grave, so take the time, if you can, to create a photographic record of the entire cemetery, rather than just a single tombstone.

Take at least two shots of each headstone, one close-up so that you can read the inscription and one from a distance which identifies the marker's location in the cemetery. If the gravestone is one of several in a family grouping, then you may also want to take a wide-angle shot of the entire family plot (a tombstone's position in relation to other family members may provide a clue to relationships).

Take several pictures from different angles showing the entire cemetery, or at least as large a portion of it as you can fit in a single picture.

Unless it is a small family plot hidden in the middle of a cornfield, the front gates or entrance of the cemetery makes another good view to record digitally or on film.

It is not always as easy as it seems, however, to achieve sharp, clear photographs of stones that may be centuries old. That old stone may be easy enough to read from just a few feet away, but capturing its three-dimensional carvings and inscriptions in a photograph sometimes takes a bit of work.

Proper lighting is the most critical factor in achieving a good, high-definition tombstone photo. According to tradition, many older cemeteries buried individuals facing east, which generally means that headstone inscriptions face that direction as well. Consequently, mid-morning is the best time for photographs; shooting early in the morning or late in the afternoon will likely create a shadow over the stone. However, there are exceptions to this very general rule; tombstones may be situated so that they face the road or a particular view, for instance. Overhead trees and cloudy days can also make photographing tombstones a difficult task. For this reason, it is best to scout out the cemetery in advance in order to determine the best time of day for taking pictures.

Many experts have claimed that photographs will be of higher quality if taken on an overcast day. However, it has been my experience that a very sunny day in either summer or winter is the best time for gravestone photography. However, be particularly aware of shadows from nearby tree branches and try to avoid them. What can go virtually unnoticed on site can actually leave harsh lines on the face of a photographic image, making it harder to read or decipher later.

When optimal lighting is not possible, several tools can be used to reflect light onto shadowy tombstones. Directing sunlight or other light diagonally across the face of a gravestone often makes inscriptions more visible and easy to read.

- A mirror is a common tool for reflecting sunlight onto shadowy tombstones. Mylar (plastic) mirrors are available at most home stores and can be easily equipped with a set of legs – such as an easel – to aid in effectively reflecting sunlight. Larger mirrors can even be used to reflect sunlight to light up tombstones resting under shady trees.

- A collapsible reflector is a common accessory used by many photographers and can be purchased for about $30-$50. They typically fold up into a small package, making them quite handy for traveling.

- Aluminum foil is a low-budget alternative and makes a decent light reflector. You will either need a piece of cardboard to support the foil or a partner to hold it for you.

- Finally, when good lighting just is not enough to bring out a badly-eroded inscription, simply wetting the stone with regular water can work wonders. After wetting the stone, allow the surface to dry for a few minutes, leaving the indented lettering damp, which makes it darker and easier to read.

Avoid using any other methods. Gravestones are historic artifacts and should be treated with respect. Some have been around since the 1600s. Acid-based compounds, such as vinegar, can eat away marble. Many genealogists once used shaving cream to clean the stone and bring out the image, but this practice has now been recognized as damaging to the stone. Rubbing chalk across the face of the stone is also no longer recommended, as it can leave a residue on porous stones and create fine scratch marks.

When returning home, take time to keep proper records. Fill out cemetery transcription forms. Printed photos should be attached to any information about a particular stone. The style and composition of the stone should be noted. If you have taken a rubbing, note this and attach a copy.

The who, what, when, where and why should always be included. Be sure to include in your notes information about the condition of the stone, repairs that have been made or that you are considering doing yourself. If it has been repaired, consider the quality of the work. Personal observations and thoughts about the gravestone and cemetery should also be included. Remember: stones are history books in mineral form. They should be treated as such.

CEMETERY NAME _____ DATE _____ RESEARCHER _____

DECEASED INFORMATION
1. Name on headstone _____
2. Year of birth _____
3. Year of death _____
4. Age at death _____
5. Historical Era
   - ☐ Pioneer (1700s-1879)
   - ☐ Victorian (1880-1905)
   - ☐ Conservative (1905-1929)
   - ☐ Modern (1930-1970)
   - ☐ Present (1971-present)

GRAVE MARKER INFORMATION
1. Design category/categories ...
   - ☐ Obelisk
   - ☐ Ground/Lawn Marker
   - ☐ Scroll
   - ☐ Raised Top
   - ☐ Wall Vault
   - ☐ Table or Box Tomb
   - ☐ Die/Base/Cap
   - ☐ Die On Base
   - ☐ Die In Socket
   - ☐ Pedestal - Urn
   - ☐ Pedestal - Vaulted Top
   - ☐ Column
   - ☐ Pulpit
   - ☐ Block Marker
   - ☐ Sarcophagus
   - ☐ Crypt
   - ☐ Plaque Marker
   - ☐ Tablet
   - ☐ Headstone Only
   - ☐ Ledger
   - ☐ Military Issue
   - ☐ Bedstead
   - ☐ Family Plot Elements (fence/gates/etc.)
   - ☐ Other (describe) _____

2. Symbols ...
   - ☐ Religious
   - ☐ Animal(s)
   - ☐ Child Image/Theme
   - ☐ Eternal Life
   - ☐ Trade/Occupation
   - ☐ Plant(s)
   - ☐ Mortality
   - ☐ Military
   - ☐ Hands
   - ☐ Organization(s)
   - ☐ Other (describe) _____

3. Inscription
   - ☐ Mint
   - ☐ Hard to read
   - ☐ Worn smooth
   - ☐ Clear but worn
   - ☐ Words apparent, can't read

4. Evidence of Human-made Damage
   - ☐ Vandalism   ☐ Graffiti   ☐ None

5. Evidence of Natural Weathering
   - ☐ Fracturing/Cracking   ☐ Parting
   - ☐ Chipping/Flaking   ☐ Sheeting
   - ☐ None

6. Evidence of Chemical Weathering
   - ☐ Dissolution   ☐ Oxidation
   - ☐ Hydrolysis   ☐ Biological Effects
   - ☐ None

GEOGRAPHICAL INFORMATION
1. Location of cemetery ...
   - ☐ Rural
   - ☐ Suburban
   - ☐ Urban

2. Plot layout of cemetery ...
   - ☐ Congruent square block grid
   - ☐ Non-congruent square block grid
   - ☐ Paths curve and follow land shape
   - ☐ Grid and curve
   - ☐ Random

3. Section of cemetery where grave is located ...
   - ☐ North   ☐ South
   - ☐ East   ☐ West
   - ☐ Northeast   ☐ Southeast
   - ☐ Northwest   ☐ Southwest

4. Placement of grave in cemetery ...
   - ☐ Near side or edge   ☐ Near front
   - ☐ Near center   ☐ Near back

5. Direction grave is facing ...
   - ☐ North   ☐ South
   - ☐ East   ☐ West
   - ☐ Northeast   ☐ Southeast
   - ☐ Northwest   ☐ Southwest

Cemetery Transcription Form

Name of Researcher: _____ **Date:** _____

Name of Cemetery: _____

Location of Cemetery: _____

_____

Grave Marker Description	Grave Marker Inscription
Headstone: Footstone: Symbols/Images/Art: Decorations/Objects of Rembrance:	
Headstone: Footstone: Symbols/Images/Art: Decorations/Objects of Rembrance:	
Headstone: Footstone: Symbols/Images/Art: Decorations/Objects of Rembrance:	
Headstone: Footstone: Symbols/Images/Art: Decorations/Objects of Rembrance:	

Attach additional notes, photographs or rubbings, if available.

SACRED
to the memory of
WILLIAM H. MOSELY
Died Sept. 10, 1854
Aged 52 years
Also his Son
WILLIAM H. MOSELY
Died May 1, 1865
Aged 23 years
May they rest in peace
Also his grand Sons
SAMUEL & CHARLES HOOVER

CHAPTER 4

Stone

IDENTIFICATION

Many common gravestone characteristics exist.

Here are the most common stone types in American graveyards, based on the order in which they were predominately used:

SLATE (1650-1900) – METAMORPHOSIS SHALE

This was the earliest stone used extensively in the Boston area, which was the hub of American gravestone carving activity from approximately 1660 to 1800. Luckily, the area boasted a supply of very high-quality slate to carve into stones. Many still survive and are most often a gray color. They tend to be thinner than marble, but most are unaffected by acid rain. Inscriptions tend to be shallow but are often readable nevertheless. Good examples are in Boston, where many of the oldest gravestones are composed of slate.

SANDSTONE OR BROWNSTONE (1650- 1890) – SEDIMENTARY ROCK & COMPRESSED SAND

Sandstone was the most commonly used stone throughout the Connecticut River Valley. Most brownstone quarries in America were in Connecticut. Sandstone was transported via railroads during the later part of the 1800s throughout the eastern United States and beyond. The color ranges from a dark blonde to varying shades of brown. It tends to delaminate, or separate, along its bedding planes. Brownstone can deteriorate quickly, turning back into the sand from which it was formed.

Marble or Limestone (1780-1930) – Sedimentary Rock & Compressed Shells

This stone of choice was the most desired in its purest white form. Marble was white with a satin finish when first installed in graveyards; limestone was usually darker and tended toward gray. Both are composed of calcium carbonate, and are therefore adversely affected by acid rain. Once weathered, they may be hard to read and are likely to be stained and darker in color than when new. The surface is likely to be pitted to some degree. Marble was most common throughout the 1800s, but was also used as early as the late 1700s and on into the early 1900s.

Granite (1860- Present Day) - Igneous Rock & Liquid Rock

Granite is by far the most durable of all natural rock. One of the strongest and longest lasting materials that exist in nature, it more than earns its sobriquet "Rock of Ages." Commonly a gray color, some regions across the country produce distinctly colored granites. It is considered the dominant stone of today and is used throughout the world in cemeteries because of its exceptional strength and permanence. Many modern cemeteries allow only granite headstones and markers to be installed. Through extensive world trade, granite is now widely available.

Styles of Gravestones

Gravestones have distinctive styles and materials depending on the year in which they were made:

Pre-1800: Slender, square sandstone or slate slabs with or without elaborate carvings.

1830-1860: Moderate sculptured stones of white marble subject to lichen moss.

1860-1880: Square, towering marble stones often elaborately shaped or with ornate sculpture.

1800-1910: Soft, gray granite stone subject to weathering.

1910-present: Polished granite or marble, sometimes lying flat.

By studying the vintage of the tombstone, the researcher can more accurately determine the validity of its inscription. Modern stones with ancient dates indicate replacement of an earlier stone or time lapse between death and grave marker. The date the stone was placed on the grave is important. One placed two days after the funeral is more accurate than one erected decades later.

In 1873, Secretary of War William W. Belknap adopted the first design for stones to be erected in national cemeteries. For the unknown dead, the stone was a block of white marble or durable stone six inches square and 30 inches deep. The top and four inches of the upper sides were finished and the number of the grave cut on the top. The use of stone blocks for marking unknown graves in national cemeteries was later discontinued, and graves were thereafter marked with the same design as those furnished for the known dead.

The War Department adopted a slab design of marble or durable stone four inches thick, 10 inches wide and 12 inches in height extending above the ground. The portion above the ground was polished and the top slightly curved. The number of the grave, rank, name of the soldier and the name of the state were cut on the front face. This original design for the permanent headstone is referred to as the Civil War type and was originally furnished for members of the Union Army only.

The stone featured a sunken shield in which the inscription appeared in bas relief. On February 3, 1879, Congress authorized the furnishing of stones for the unmarked graves of veterans in private cemeteries.

The Civil War era headstone was furnished not only for the unmarked graves of that war, but also for the unmarked graves of eligible deceased soldiers of the American Revolution, War of 1812, Mexican War, Indian Campaigns and later, the Spanish-American War.

The question of permanently marking the graves of Confederate deceased in national cemeteries and Confederate burial plots resulted in an

act of March 9, 1906, authorizing the furnishing of headstones for the graves of Confederates who died, primarily in Union prison camps and were buried in federal cemeteries.

Congress adopted the same size and material for Confederate headstones as for those of other wars. The design varied in that the top was pointed instead of rounded and the shield was omitted. An act of February 26, 1929, authorized the furnishing of this type of stone for graves in private cemeteries.

Following World War I, a board of officers composed of Assistant Secretary of War J.M. Wainwright, Army Chief of Staff General John J. Pershing and Quartermaster General Harry L. Rogers adopted a new design to be used for all graves except those of veterans of the Civil and Spanish-American Wars.

This stone was of the slab design referred to as the General type, slightly rounded at the top, made of American white marble and standing 42 inches long, 13 inches wide and four inches thick. The inscription on the front face would include the name, rank, regiment, division, date of death and home state of the fallen.

For the first time a religious emblem was authorized for use only on the general type stone. The choice of emblem was limited to the Latin Cross for the Christian faith and the Star of David for Judaism.

Glossary of Common Gravestone Symbols & Interpretations

Following are some of the most commonly encountered symbolic icons & carvings, along with their accepted and defined meanings.

BIRDS

Birds in flight are symbolic of the "winged soul." The representation of the soul by a bird goes back to ancient Egypt. Some older burial art features only wings to convey the symbol of divine mission. Wings or birds often denote graves of children or represent eternal life.

Dove - An important symbolic animal in Christianity representing the Holy Spirit. The white dove is referred to in the story of baptism of Christ: "And John bore record, saying, I saw the Spirit descending from heaven like a dove, and it abode upon him" (John 1:32). The descending dove is a very common motif on grave memorials. Seven doves are representative of the seven spirits of God or the Holy Spirit in its sevenfold gift of grace. Purity, devotion, divine spirit. A dove with an olive sprig means peace, hope or promise.

Eagle -Suggests courage and possibly a military career symbol for Saint John.

Owl - Suggests wisdom.

Rooster - Awakening; resurrection.

Swallow - Indicates a child or motherhood.

Butterfly - Represents the soul; although rare, it is occasionally seen on graves, usually those of children. Also symbolic of resurrection, a meaning derived from the three stages of the life of the butterfly – the caterpillar, the chrysalis, and the butterfly. The three stages are symbols of life, death and resurrection.

ANIMALS

Many grave memorials display incised or three-dimensional animals, and these have strong symbolic meanings.

Dog - Signifies loyalty and that the master was worth loving.

Dolphin - Portrays the idea of resurrection.

Dragon - Being defeated by St. George, depicts triumph over sin.

Fish - Indicates Christian faith.

Frog - Depicts sin and worldly pleasures, or may represent resurrection.

Hart - Male deer; represents either faithfulness, thirsting for God, or Christ slaying Satan.

Horse - Courage or generosity; an attribute of St. George, St. Martin, St. Maurice and St. Victor, all of whom are represented in Christian art on horseback.

Lamb - This is the most common animal symbol found on a child's grave. The lamb appears throughout the ages with great regularity in Christian art and because it is a symbol of Christ. The use of the lamb in religious art pre-dates Christianity and appears to have been used first by the Egyptians. It signifies purity, innocence, and Christ in his sacrificial role, personifying gentleness and humility.

Lion - Symbolizes the power of God and guards the tomb against evil spirits; like other guardians, the lion's watch is as eternal as the stone of which it is depicted. The lion also recalls the courage and determination of the souls they guard; manifests the spirit of the departed.

Peacock - Signifies the incorruptibility of flesh, resurrection, beauty of soul, immortality.

Phoenix - Represents the incorruptibility of flesh, resurrection, beauty of soul, immortality.

Serpent - Symbolizes eternity when swallowing its own tail.

Squirrel with a nut - Signifies religious meditation or spiritual striving.

ARMS, HANDS & HEART

Arms outstretched - A plea for mercy.

Eye of God/All-Seeing Eye - Symbolizes an all-knowing and ever-present God. During the European Renaissance, it was common to illustrate the Eye of God surrounded by a triangle representing the Holy Trinity. The eye within the triangle surrounded by a circle and radiating rays of light has been used to symbolize the holiness of the true God.

Hands - Hands in some form are quite common on graves.

- **Hands clasped**: At first glance, these hands all seem to be in the same fashion but a number of interesting characteristics stand out. First, most of the hands illustrate the right hand in a grasp with fingers overlapping the other hand while the left hand is open. This could be the depiction of a man holding a woman's hand and indicate marriage, a close bond between individuals, or unity and affection even after

death. Clasped hands are also symbolic of a farewell or final goodbye. Look at the cuff to distinguish between a man and woman's hand. The person who died first holds the other's hand, guiding the spouse to heaven.

- **Hand of God**: When plucking a chain, represents God bringing a soul unto Himself.
- **Hands holding an object**: Holding a *chain* with a broken link symbolizes the death of a family member; holding a *heart* represents charity and is common on 19th Century memorials (typically seen on memorials of members of the Independent Order of Odd Fellows, a charity); holding an *open book* signifies the embodiment of faith.
- **Hand pointing**: *Downward* symbolizes mortality or sudden death, and is possibly a depiction of a secret Masonic handshake; *upward* refers to the reward of the righteous, confirmation of life after death.
- **Hands praying**: Signifies devotion.

Heart - Love, mortality, love of God, courage and intelligence.
- **Bleeding**: Christ's suffering for followers' sins.
- **Encircled with thorns**: The suffering of Christ.
- **Flaming**: Signifies extreme religious fervor.
- **Pierced by a sword**: The Virgin Mary, harkening to Simeon's prophecy to Mary at the birth of Christ: "Yea, a sword shall pierce through thine own soul"; also used to represent charity.

GEOMETRIC SYMBOLISM

Geometric forms are commonly found on grave memorials, various forms of the cross being one of the most widely-used shapes.

Cross - The ties between religious beliefs and symbolism have always been strong. To Christians, the greatest symbolic message is in the crucifix. The crucifix or cross can generate many symbolic messages ranging from love, faith and goodness (taught by Jesus, who was crucified on a cross) to terror and fear (the Ku-Klux-Klan's use of the burning cross to harass and threaten). There are many types of Christian crosses worldwide, and a few are common in North America. Here are some cross designs that are often encountered in cemeteries and on gravestones:

- **Cross with circle:** While Christianity has adopted its original symbolic meaning, the circle is pre-Christian. It is universally known as the symbol of eternity and never-ending existence. Extremely common on gravesites, its usual representation is of a cross surrounded by a circle. Two circles, one above the other, represent earth and sky (or heaven). Three interconnected circles represent the Holy Trinity.
- **Botonee Cross:** Its modified trefoil or three-lobed ends represents the trinity.
- **Calvary Cross**: A Latin cross standing on three steps or blocks, it signifies faith, hope and love. Love is sometimes replaced by charity.

- **Celtic Cross** (or **Irish Cross**): The circle around the crosspiece symbolizes eternity. Its origin can be traced to the Celtic cultures of the British Isles. One legend tells of how St. Patrick while preaching was shown a sacred standing stone that was marked with a circle that was symbolic of the moon goddess. Patrick made the mark of a Latin cross through the circle and blessed the stone making the first Celtic cross. Protestants usually call it the Celtic Cross, while Catholics often refer to it as an Irish Cross. This cross is sometimes used to mark the graves of priests or monks.

- **Eastern Cross:** Used in the Russian and Greek Orthodox traditions, this cross includes an upper horizontal mark representing the inscription over the head of Jesus. A lower slanting mark represents the footrest of the crucified Jesus.
- **Eye of God surrounded by a triangle and a circle:** Symbolic of the eternity of the Holy Trinity.
- **Fleuree Cross/Gothic Cross:** This flowered cross symbolizes the adult Christian by its more opened, flared-outward style.
- **Greek Cross:** It has four arms equal in length and is the traditional symbol of Christian faith. The equal length drawing of the cross is pre-Christian, and in paganism, represents the four elements – earth, air, fire and water. The International Red Cross uses this symbol.

- **Ionic Cross:** Similar to the Celtic cross, its ends flair outward. The ionic cross signifies everlasting salvation, love and glory. The circle around the crosspiece symbolizes eternity.
- **Latin Cross / Western Cross:** One of the oldest symbols of Christianity and the most commonly used form, it is also the simplest in design. In early times, it was called God's mark

- **St. Andrew's Cross:** This is an X-shaped cross. Legend tells that when St. Andrew was martyred, he could not bear to be crucified on the same style of cross on which Christ had died, so he requested this shape be built for his execution.
- **St. Anthony's Cross:** T-shaped; also known as the Old Testament cross.

Triangle/Trefoil/Triquetra - In Christianity, the equilateral triangle is the symbol of the Trinity. Other geometric shapes representing the Holy Trinity are the trefoil, the triquetra, the circle within the triangle, the triangle in a circle, and the triquetra and circle. To the ancient Egyptians, the triangle was an emblem of Godhead; to the Pythagoreans, it symbolized wisdom. Another use is found in the symbol of the eye of God surrounded by a triangle.

Swastika - Exact origin is unknown, but this is considered one of the oldest symbols used. Commonly found on Buddhist memorials, it represents the seal of the Buddha's heart; the doctrine of Buddha; the round of existence. To the Chinese, the swastika had two forms symbolizing the male and female, clockwise and anti-clockwise. Also used by the Romans and, much later, by the Nazis in Germany during the World War II era.

Square - It represents the earth and earthly existence. Some monuments have a cube or square inverted to point the corners downward and upward. This illustrates earthly existence and the directions of earth and heaven.

Pentagram - This is a five-pointed, star-shaped figure made by extending the sides of a regular pentagon until they meet. This figure pre-dates Christianity and is believed to have first been used by Pythagoras, the Greek mathematician and theorist. Later in the Middle Ages, the pentagram was used by magicians and sorcerers. It was believed that the pentagram offered protection against evil. Christianity adopted the figure and the symbolism to suggest the five wounds suffered by Christ on the cross. It is interesting to note that the pentagram is used by both Christians and Wiccans.

Pyramid - Symbolizes eternity. It was supposed that a pyramid-shaped tombstone prevented the devil from reclining on a grave.

STARS

Five-pointed pentagram star - A five-pointed star is symbolic of the life of Christ and may also represent the five wounds of Christ. This star is drawn with one stroke of the pen. Its exact origin is unknown, and its meaning has changed throughout the ages. The pre-Christian Celtic priests called it the witch's foot. It is also called Solomon's Seal and was known in the Middle Ages as the goblin's cross. Today the symbol is a favorite among graffiti artists, as well as so-called demonology practitioners. Like the pentagon, it is believed to have protective powers against evil. In Wiccan belief, it represents protection against demons and a symbol of safety. The ancient Babylonians used the symbol as a magic charm. The five-pointed pentagram star represents the five senses. To the Jews, it represents the five mosaic books. This symbol has also been adopted by Masonic organizations (e.g., the Eastern Star).

The Star of David - Six-pointed star or Star of David, also known as *Magen David* (Hebrew for *shield of David*), it is typically used as a symbol of Judaism. The star is actually made of two triangles. It signifies

divine protection as epitomized by the alchemistic signs for fire and water, which are an upward and downward apex triangle. The star is a very ancient symbol, used by several Asia Minor cultures, as well as some Greek city states. In Jewish culture, the Star of David came into widespread use at the beginning of the 20th Century.

OBJECTS

Anchor - Early Christians used the anchor as a disguised cross and as a marker to guide the way to secret meeting places. A Christian symbol of hope, it is found as funerary symbolism in the art of the catacombs. Often set amongst rocks, it can also be an occupational symbol in seafaring areas or the attribute of St. Nicholas, patron saint of seamen, signifying hope and steadfastness. An anchor with a broken chain stands for the cessation of life.

Arch - Victory of life or victory in death.

Arrow - Denotes mortality.

Angels - The agent of God, often pointing towards heaven. Guardians of the dead, symbolizing spirituality. Angels are shown in all types of poses with different symbolism. Angels are sometimes seen carrying the departed soul of a child in their arms or as a Guardian embracing the dead. These "messengers of god" are often shown escorting the deceased to heaven. Two angels can be named, and are identified by the objects they carry: Michael, who bears a sword, and Gabriel, who is depicted with a horn representing the Day of Judgment and the Resurrection. If they are pictured flying, it typically symbolizes rebirth. Many angels gathered in the clouds refers to heaven. If they are shown weeping, it signifies mourning an untimely death.

Baby's chair - Small, empty furniture symbolizes unfulfilled lives of children, representing the child now gone. Small shoes on the chair refer to the inability to achieve adulthood.

Bible - Represents a religious layperson or a cleric.

Book - Refers to a literate person, a scholar. Can represent faith. It is sometimes interpreted as a prayer, knowledge or even memory, particularly when it has a dog-eared page. A book may also represent the Book of Life. A popular form is the book as a double-page spread.

Candle with a Flame - Life.

Chalice – Sacraments.

Cherubs - Graves of children.

Cherub's Head - The soul.

Children - A child represents the untimely death of the innocent; may be shown mourning a parent; holding a skull means they are dead themselves.

Chrisma - A cross-like shape formed by a combination of two Greek letters, *chi* (X) and *rho* (P) corresponding to C, H and R of the word *Christ*.

Circle – Signifies perfection or eternity in the afterlife.

Coffin or Sarcophagus monument - Mortality.

Column, broken - An early grief, end of life, sorrow; life cut short too soon. May be girded with flowers, representing decay; usually represents the loss of the head of a family.

Columns, with archway - Heavenly entrance.

Cross and Anchor - Another early Christian symbol referring to Christ as "hope we have as an anchor of the soul, both sincere and steadfast" (Hebrews 6:19).

Crown - Immortality, righteousness, victory, triumph, resurrection; symbolic of honor or glory of life after death. May be shown being offered to those on earth by angels.

Crown on a cross - Sovereignty of the Lord.

Death's Head - The most common symbol on early American gravestones warning those above ground that they may be next to die. Very common from the earliest American stones of the late 17th Century until the soul effigy became more popular in the mid-18th Century.

Doors and gates - Passage into the afterlife; heavenly entrance.

Drapery over anything - Sorrow; mourning.

Flame - Eternity.

Grim Reaper - Death personified.

Harp - Associated with David in the Old Testament; symbol of St. Cecilia, patron saint of musicians; symbolizes worship in heaven and hope.

Hourglass - Signifies the inevitable passing of time and the shortness of life; an attribute of death and Father Time. If depicted on its side, the hourglass symbolizes that time has stopped for the deceased.

Keys - Spiritual knowledge or, held in the hands of an angel or saint, a means to enter heaven.

Knot - The interlaced Celtic knot represents resurrection and life everlasting.

Labyrinth - The passage of life.

Lamp - Knowledge; a love of learning; the immortality of the spirit.

Menorah - This Jewish symbol for divine presence of God is a seven-branched candlestick.

Pale, Pick, Spade - Mortality.

Pitcher - A traditional Jewish symbol referencing the Levites; if depicted with an ewer, it signifies washing the hands of the High Priests.

Rod or staff - Comfort.

Scroll - Symbolizes life and time. Both ends rolled up indicates a life that is unfolding like a scroll of uncertain length with the past and future hidden. Often shown being held by a hand representing life being recorded by angels. It can also suggest honor and commemoration.

Scythe - Death, the divine harvest.

Shell - The use of shell in burials is pre-Christian in practice and pre-dates even Egyptian burial practices. The shell is symbolic of fertility, resurrection and pilgrimage. Shells, coins and small stones are traditional remembrance objects left at gravesites. There are several meanings given to this act – a symbolic referral to the ancient custom of burying the dead under a cairn of rocks to protect the body from scavenging animals or a reminder that the individual is not forgotten.

Scallop - Symbol of the Crusades, pilgrims, pilgrims' journey, resurrection, life everlasting and one's life journey. It was a traditional symbol of the Puritans.

Ship - The grave of a seafarer.

Sickle - Death as the last harvest.

Skull, skeleton - Mortality; death.

Star - Represents the spirit, piercing the darkness as an expression of triumph over the overwhelming odds of oblivion. Five-pointed stars signify the spirit rising to heaven.

Sun setting - Death.

Sun shining/rising - Renewed life.

Sword - A military career.

Swords, crossed - Indicates death in battle.

Torch - Lit or upright torch represents life; inverted or extinguished torch means death.

Trumpets - Victory and resurrection.

Urn - Greek symbol of mourning, the body as a vessel of the soul, originating as a repository for the ashes of the dead in ancient times. Most urns represent an ossuary. In several examples an angel is looking inside it as if to inspect the contents. A flame is sometimes shown coming from the urn. They often appear draped with a cloth – usually representing the death of an elderly person – or festooned with a wreath or garland. This fashion of urns persisted well into the 1850s.

Urn & Willow - The most common of all Victorian symbols found on a large portion of gravestones throughout the 19th Century; also associated with the Greek Revival, symbolizing the mourning of the deceased.

Vessel with flame - The eternal flame or the eternal spirit of humankind.

Winged face - Effigy of the deceased's soul.

Winged globe - A symbol of the Egyptian sun god, Re; on Victorian monuments it is symbolic of the power that can recreate and means "God, Lord over all, creator."

Winged skull - Flight of the soul from mortal man.

Winged wheel - Symbolizes the Holy Spirit.

Woman with or without Bible pointing upward - Faith.

Woman clinging to a cross - Signifies faith; originates from a drawing that accompanied the hymn "Rock of Ages." Also sometimes seen as a woman clinging to a pillar or anchor. A common motif on white bronze monuments and Masonic grave memorials.

PLANTS

Flowers convey love, grief, happiness and other emotions. They may be the most common icon or motif you will see in a cemetery. These symbolic connections of flowers with emotion are cross-cultural, but their origins are generally unknown. The ancient Greeks sometimes planted flowers in cemeteries. In addition, evidence of flowers has been found in some Neanderthal tombs. During the 1800s, the use of floral symbolism became so popular that almost every flower known had a meaning attached to it. Here are some symbolic references related to common plants and flowers:

Acacia - Immortality of soul.

Acanthus - Heavenly garden. One of the oldest cemetery motifs, acanthus is associated with the rocky ground where most ancient Greek cemeteries were placed. It is a common motif found on memorials, especially since Acanthus leaves are used to decorate the capital of a Corinthian column.

Bamboo - The emblem of Buddha. The seven-knotted bamboo denotes the seven degrees of initiation and invocation in Buddhism. On Japanese memorials, it symbolizes devotion and truthfulness.

Buttercup - Cheerfulness.

Calla lily - Marriage.

Cinquefoil - Maternal affection; beloved daughter.

Corn - Often an occupational symbol, it was a country custom to send a sheaf to relatives on the death of a farmer.

Crocus - Youthful gladness.

Cypress tree - Hope.

Daisy - Innocence of child; Jesus the Infant.

Dead leaves - Sadness; melancholy.

Dogwood - Christianity; divine sacrifice; eternal life; resurrection.

Fern - Sincerity; sorrow.

Figs - Prosperity; eternal life.

Fleur-de-lis - Flame; passion; ardor; mother.

Flower - Frailty of life.

Broken flower - A life terminated; mortality.

Forget-me-not - Remembrance.

Ivy - Memory; immortality; friendship; fidelity; faithfulness; undying affection; eternal life.

Grapes - Christ.

Grapes and Leaves - Christian faith.

Hawthorn - Hope; happiness; springtime.

Holly - Foresight.

Honeysuckle - Bonds of love; generosity; devoted affection.

Lalla - Beauty; marriage.

Laurel leaves - Special achievement; distinction; success; triumph.

Lily - Majesty; innocence; purity; resurrection. Often associated with the Virgin Mary. Usually used on women's graves. Their use at funerals symbolizes the restored innocence of the soul at death.

Lily of the valley - Return of happiness; purity; humility.

Morning glory - Resurrection; mourning; youth; farewell; brevity of life; mortality.

Mystic rose - Mother.

Moss - Merit.

Mulberry - Mortality.

Oak tree - Hospitality; stability; strength; honor; eternity; endurance; liberty. It is believed by some to have been the tree from which Christ's cross was made. In small pioneer cemeteries, it is common to place children's graves near oak trees. The oak tree was the tree of life in pre-Christian times. The Druids worshiped the oak. The oak, oak leaves and acorn can stand for power, authority or victory; sometimes seen on military tombs.

Passion flower - The elements of the passion of Christ: the lacy crown is the crown of thorns; the five stamens are the five wounds; the 10 petals are the 10 Apostles who remained faithful.

Pineapple - Hospitality; good host.

Palm - Spiritual victory; success; eternal peace; symbol of Christ's victory associated with Easter.

Pansy - Remembrance; humility.

Pine - Fertility; regeneration; fidelity.

Poppy - Peace; rest; eternal sleep; consolation.

Rose - Beauty; hope; unfailing love; associated with the Virgin Mary, the "rose without thorns." During the Victorian Age, roses had a unique representation for women and young girls. A red rose symbolizes martyrdom, and a white rose symbolizes purity and virginity. The maturation of the rose often indicates how old the person was at the time of death, normally a child twelve or under. A broken rosebud or a rose in partial bloom represents a teenager. Full bloom refers to the person dying in the prime of life, normally in their early to mid-twenties. Joined rosebuds symbolize a strong bond between two people (e.g., mother and child who died at the same time). Several rosebuds on the same branch represent secrecy. A rosette references the Lord, messianic hope and promise. A wreath of roses signifies beauty and virtue rewarded.

Shamrock - Symbolic of Ireland (country of origin).

Thistle - Earthly sorrow; Christ's crown of thorns; symbolic of Scotland (country of origin).

Tree - The Tree of Life; the all-covering love of Christ.

Severed branch - Mortality.

Vine - The sacraments; God's blood.

Weeping Willow - Nature's lament; sorrow and mourning.

Wheat - Resurrection; bread and wine (Christian); fertility.

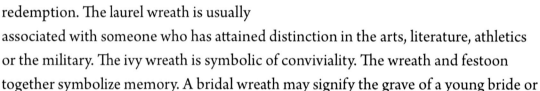
A bushel signifies the body of Christ. Sheaves represent the divine harvest or the elderly.

Wreath or Garland - The use of garlands, wreaths and festoons dates back to ancient Greeks and was adopted by the Christian religion as a symbol of victory and redemption. The laurel wreath is usually associated with someone who has attained distinction in the arts, literature, athletics or the military. The ivy wreath is symbolic of conviviality. The wreath and festoon together symbolize memory. A bridal wreath may signify the grave of a young bride or groom. Conversely, a maiden's garland was often carried at funerals of unmarried women with blameless reputations. Garlands of white paper or linen, embellished with streamers and a single white glove, were hung in the church after the funeral and allowed to decay. The pieces would then be buried in the graveyard.

Yew tree - Sadness

acc. - according to

acco. - account

accu. - accurate

adj. - adjoining

adm. - admission or admitted

admin. - administration

aft. - after

alleg. - allegiance

ano. - another

approx. - approximately

ar. co. - artillery company

a.s. - died in the year of his/her age (*anno aetitis suae*)

ascert. - ascertained

b. - born or birth

bapt. - baptized or baptism

bec. - because or became

bef. - before

bot. - bought or bottom

br. - brother

bur. - buried

capt. - captain, captured or captivity

catal. - catalog

ch. - child, children or church

clk. - clerk

Co. - county or company

Col. - colony or Colonel

Coll. - college or collections

comp. - company

confer. - conferred

conject. - conjecture

cont. - continued

contr. - contract

corp. - Corporal

couns. - counselor

cous. - cousin

coven. - covenant

ct. - court

d. - died, death or daughter

deac. - deacon

decis. - decision

degr. - degree

devis. - devised

discip. - discipline

div. - division or divided

docum. - document

d.s.p. - died without issue

d.s.p.l. - died without legitimate issue (*decessit sine prole legitima*)

d.s.p.m.s. - died without surviving male issue (*decessit sine prole mascula supersita*)

d.s.p.s. - died without surviving issue (*decessit sine prole supersita*)

d.unm. - died unmarried

d.v.p. - died in the lifetime of his father (*decessit vita patris*)

d.v.m. - died in the lifetime of his mother (*decessit vita matris*)

easi. - easily

educ. - education or educated

Eng. - England

eno. - enough

ens. - ensign

ensu. - ensuing

est. - estate or establish

establ. - establishment

et. al. - and others (*et alia*)

exc. - except

f. - father

fam. - family

fidel. - fidelity

foll. - following or followed

freem. - freeman or freemen

giv. - given or giving

gr. - grand, great, grant or graduate

g.f. - grandfather

gr.mo. - grandmother

gr.s. - grandson

hist. - history or historian

hon. - honorable

honor. - honorary

honora. - honorable

ign. - ignorant

Ind. - Indians

inf. - infant or informed

inhab. - inhabitant

inq. - inquiry

ins. - insert

inst. - present month (*instans*)

inv. - inventory or invitation

judic. - judicial or judicious

k. - killed or king

kn. - known

ld. -land

liber. - book or volume

Lieut. - Lieutenant

liv. - lived or living

m. - married or marriage

Maj. - Major

mak. - making

ment. - mentioned

milit. - military

min. - minister

nam. - named

N.E. - New England

not. - noted

nunc. - nuncupative (oral) will, written by a witness.

o. - oath

ob. - he/she died (*obit*)

O.E. - Old England

offic. - official

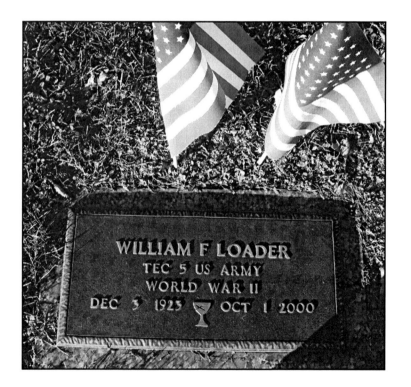

oft. - often

ord. - ordained

orig. - origin

peo. - people

petitn. - petition

preced. - preceded or preceding

pro. - probate or proved

prob. - probable or probably

prop. - property

propound. - propounded

propr. - proprietor(s)

provis. - provision

pub. - public

rat. - rated

rec. - record

rep. - report or representative

repud. - repudiated

respectiv. - respectively

r.i.p. - rest in peace

s. - son(s)

scatt. - scatter or scattered

sec. - second

Sgt. - Sergeant

sett. - settler(s)

serv. - service or servant(s)

sh. - share or ship

sis. - sister

spell. - spelled or spelling

surg. - surgeon

sw. - swear or swore

syl. - syllable

tak. - taken

tho. - though

thot. - thought

thro. - through

transcr. - transcribed

unit. - united or uniting

unm. - unmarried

var. - various or variation

w. - wife

wh. - who or which

wks. - weeks

wid. - widow

yr. - year

Latin abbreviations are especially common in Catholic cemeteries:

ad patres - to the fathers (dead or gone away)

anno aetatis suae (A.A.S.) - in the year of her/his age

anno Domini (A.D.) - in the year of our Lord

annos vixit (a.v.) - he/she lived [so many years]

beatae memoriae (B.M.) - of blessed memory

Dei gratia - by the grace of God

Dei gratias - thanks be to God

Deo, Optimo, Maximo (D.O.M.) - to God, the Best, the Greatest (motto of the Benedictine order)

Domino, Optimo, Maximo (D.O.M.) - the Lord, the Best, the Greatest (alternate motto)

gloria in Excelsis Deo - glory be to God, the Most High

hic iacet or *hic jacet (H.I.)* - here lies (Ancient Latin has no letter "J": the letter was changed later)

hic iacet sepultus (H.I.S.) - here lies buried

hic sepultus (H.S.) - here is buried

Iesus Nazarenus, Rex Iudaeorum (I.N.R.I.) - Jesus Christ, King of the Jews

in hoc salus (I.H.S.) - there is safety in this

in hoc signo spes mea (I.H.S.) - in this sign (the cross of Christ) is my hope

in hoc signos vinces (I.H.S.) - by this sign you will conquer

laus Deo - praise be to God

memento mori - remember you must die; remember thy death

obit (ob.) - he/she died

requiescat in pace (R.I.P.) - may she/he rest in peace

requiescant in pace (R.I.P.) - may they rest in peace

Verbi Dei Minister (V.D.M.) - Minister of the Word of God

Pedestal Tomb - Vaulted Top

Box Tomb

Table Tomb

Obelisk (draped)

Pedestal Tomb - Urn

Pulpit Marker

Raised Top

Lawn Marker

Plaque Marker

Headstone

Footstone

Bedstead

Ledger

**Gov't Issue - Civil War
Confederate**

**Gov't Issue - Civil War Union
& Spanish American War**

Gov't Issue - General

Die in Socket

Die on Base

Die, Base & Cap

CHAPTER 5

Gravestone

WEATHERING & REPAIR

Environmental conditions affect gravestones.

Before trying your hand at preservation, you should observe how the stone is handling the weathering process.

Weathering

Granular disintegration is occurring when the surface has a "sugary" feel. Just as a sugar cube melts when touched with water, the mineral grains of the stone will be visible as protruding forms on the surface. Some of the inscription might have "melted away" – the lettering will become less distinctive.

When stone fragments of varying sizes detach themselves from the surface of the stone, **flaking** is in process. Similarly, **blistering** is taking place when a domed or raised surface appears on the gravestone. If tapped, the dome will sound hollow. Over time, it will burst and flake away from the central dome. The inside of the blister may appear to be composed of more friable material.

Contour weathering occurs when an entire surface breaks away from the gravestone as a single sheet. The sheet tends to follow the contours of the underlying carved form.

Pitting is a weathering process involving distinct depressions on the surface of the gravestone. These can be shallow or deep in form. Measurement of the pits is possible either directly using calipers to measure length, breadth and depth, or indirectly by classifying them by size (e.g., 0-1 mm, 1.1-5mm, 5.1-10 mm, 10+mm).

Black crusts are deposits often found in sheltered areas. On marble stones, these crusts often have "cauliflower" forms on a micro level. This indicates the presence of calcium sulphate, a crust formed by dry deposition. There are also likely to be deposits of soot and other particles on exposed areas.

Cleaning Gravestones

It is sometimes necessary to clean a gravestone in order to interpret it. This is not for the inexperienced, nor for those who wish instant and complete success in a short time. It takes a lot of work and patience, but the outcome can be quite satisfying. A word of caution: these procedures should only be completed at private cemeteries where there is no maintenance personnel.

EVALUATE THE GENERAL CONDITION OF THE GRAVESTONE. Do not attempt to clean the monument if it exhibits any cracks, flaking and scaling, or eroding granular surfaces. Carefully "sound" the stone (gently tap the surface with your finger) to determine if there are any underlying hollow areas. If any are detected, do not continue with cleaning and handling.

DETERMINE THE TYPE OF SOILING IN ORDER TO REMOVE IT IN THE MOST EFFECTIVE MANNER. Types of soiling include carbonaceous or sooty soiling, urban grime and dirt, organic (algae, fungi, lichens, mosses), stains (metallic, oils), and efforescence (salts).

INITIATE CLEANING PROCESS WITH THE LEAST AGGRESSIVE METHOD – a gentle clean water rinsing. If washing with water alone is not sufficient, carefully proceed with a selected material to facilitate cleaning. Choose the gentlest possible method that will achieve an acceptable level of cleanliness.

ALWAYS TEST SELECTED CLEANING METHOD(S) BEFORE GENERAL APPLICATION. Test the entire cleaning procedure in a small inconspicuous area of the monument.

PRE-WET THE GRAVESTONE WITH WATER BEFORE THE APPLICATION OF ANY CHEMICAL CLEANING SOLUTIONS. This prevents excessive penetration of the cleaning solutions and soiling into the stone, while also acting as a softening for the pollutants.

CLEAN FROM THE BOTTOM TO THE TOP OF THE GRAVESTONE TO AVOID STREAK-STAINING. Periodically rinse runoff.

ALWAYS RINSE THOROUGHLY WITH WATER. Residues from chemical cleaning solutions can create a blotchy appearance, provide mediums for bacterial action and cause staining. Do not allow cleaning solutions to dry on a monument.

NOTE: Do not assume that a cleaning procedure that is effective in one specific case is therefore applicable to all cleaning situations.

Evaluate Selected Cleaning Materials

SOAPS & DETERGENTS

1. **Soaps** (e.g., Ivory): Commercial household detergents (liquids and powders) are *not* recommended for cleaning masonry. They are rendered insoluble by calcium ions present in stone and hard water. They may also produce free alkali and fatty acid salts.

2. **Non-ionic Detergents** (e.g., Kodak Photo Flo): Non-ionic detergents are recommended for cleaning gravestones. They are electrically neutral cleaning agents that do not contain or contribute to the formation of soluble salts. They provide better wetting of the masonry surface and, therefore, may successfully facilitate the removal of general soiling. Non-ionic detergents are available from conservation, janitorial and photographic suppliers. A suggested cleaning solution is one ounce of non-ionic detergent to five gallons of water.

ACIDIC CLEANING MATERIALS

Hydrochloric acid, muriatic acid, phosphoric acid (e.g. "Lime Away," "Naval Jelly") and **oxalic acid** are *not* recommended for general cleaning of gravestones. The use of hydrochloric or muriatic acid may result in ferrous chloride (rust) staining and the deposition of soluble salts. Muriatic acid, which is readily available in hardware stores, is a raw acid. It is a by-product of processing steel and contains metallic particles that can cause ferrous staining.

ALKALINE, CORROSIVE & BIOCIDAL CLEANING MATERIALS

1. **Sodium hydroxide** (e.g., "Borax") and **sodium hypochlorite** (e.g., "Clorox," "liquid chlorine") are *not* recommended for general cleaning of stone.

2. **Calcium hydrochloride** (e.g., chlorine, "HTH," "Shock Treatment"): Calcium hydrochloride (or chlorine) may be effective for the removal of biological growth. It is a granular product that is not to be confused with "liquid chlorine" or sodium hydrochloride. Calcium hypochlorite is available from swimming pool suppliers. A suggested cleaning solution is one ounce of calcium hypochlorite to one gallon of hot water. *Note: This product should be used only when a water hose with strong water pressure is available.*

3. **Ammonium hydroxide** (e.g., household ammonia): Solutions of household ammonia are recommended for cleaning light colored stones. Ammonia may be particularly effective for the removal of biological growth. One cup of ammonia to one gallon of water is the recommended ratio.

4. **Quatemary ammoniums** (e.g., algaecides or biocides for swimming pools): Quaternary ammoniums have a slightly different chemical structure than ammonium hydroxide. They may be effective for the removal of biological growth, particularly stubborn black algae. Quaternary ammoniums are available from swimming pool suppliers and list ingredients such as alkylbenzyl trimethyl ammonium, benzyl alkyl dimethyl ammonium chlorides, or benzyl aklyl dimethyl ammonium bromides.

5. **Trisodium phosphate** (e.g., "TSP, "Calgon"): Trisodium phosphate is *not* recommended for cleaning monuments. It can cause the formation and deposition of soluble salts. "Calgon" contains trisodium phosphate and a number of additives that may be detrimental to monuments.

6. "Fantastic" all purpose cleaner, "Formula 409," "Spic and Span," "Comet" and other **abrasive cleansers**: These are *not* recommended for cleaning monuments. Avoid products containing sodium chloride, sodium sulfate, sodium carbonate, sodium bicarbonate, and ammonium carbonate, due to their ability to form and deposit soluble salts in monuments.

Miscellaneous Materials & Tools

The following items are recommended for use in cleaning procedures for masonry: soft natural bristle brushes, nylon brushes, tooth brushes, Q-tips, sponges (especially natural sponges). Wood and some plastic spatulas are also recommended. *NOTE: Never use metal brushes or scrapers or abrasive pads (e.g., Brillo, Scotchbrite) to clean monuments.*

CLEANING STONE TYPES

1. Marble and Limestone

- Water

- Non-ionic detergent (Kodak Photo-Flo)

- Household ammonia (requires rinse water and Hydrion Paper test strips for pH testing)

- Calcium hypochlorite (HTH) for biological growth retardation (requires water hose for rinsing and Hydrion Paper test strips for pH testing)

2. Slate and Other Stone
- Water

- Non-ionic detergent (Kodak Photo-Flo)

GENERAL CLEANING

1. Good water supply

2. Non-ionic detergent (Kodak Photo-Flo)

3. 1/4 oz. per 5 quarts water

4. Ammonia – 1 cup per 1gal. water (for marble only)

5. Calcium hypochlorite (granular) – 2 oz. dry per 1 gal. warm water

6. Assortment of brushes (NOT WIRE) of varying stiffness

7. Toothbrushes (firm)

8. Sponges

9. Scrapers - craft sticks or plastic putty knives

POULTICE - SOFTENING

1. Kaolin/porcelain clay (dry)

2. Glycerine (use 50/50 mixture with water)

3. Water

4. Saran Wrap and heavier plastic for wrapping

5. Tape/string to secure plastic

6. Scrapers - plastic and wood

CLEANING DON'TS

1. **No** wire brushes, metal instruments, abrasive pads (e.g., Scotchbrite, Brillo, steel wool)

2. **No** acid or acidic cleaners (especially on marble or limestone!) Acids should only be used by conservators with proper training on non-calcareous stone

3. **No** household cleaners: soap (e.g., Ivory), detergents (liquid or powder), Borax, Clorox, TSP, Calgon, Fantastik, Formula 409, Spic and Span (or any other abrasive cleaner)

REMEMBER: The use of improper cleaning materials and practices can cause serious and irreparable damage to gravestones. Make sure the stone is stable before attempting to clean it.

Numerous factors can contribute to breakage of the gravestone, monument or sculpture. While many might be tempted to blame this on deplorable acts of vandalism long chronicled in the media, the majority of breakages are due to environmental conditions and outright neglect.

Too often, tree limbs fall and shatter fragile marble gravestones into irreparable fragments – trees which were dead themselves and should have been pruned long ago. Cars crash through fences and destroy gravestones and monuments, toppling them like dominoes. Heavy lawn mowers mercilessly chip away and gash historic stones repeatedly, until they finally topple over.

Proper maintenance will go a long way toward helping preserve our heritage carved in stone. For those already damaged, there are many mending techniques in use today. For years, people relied on drilling and using bolts and metal plates to repair the stone. Mortars were used to join broken stone fragments, but they tended to be too thick, resulting in incorrectly sized surfaces. The result of these methods was unattractive gravestones. Thankfully, they are no longer recommended.

Mending epoxies have evolved in recent years and have enhanced the quality of gravestone conservation. The fragments of a broken gravestone can usually be joined together, provided the stone itself has enough structural integrity intact. For the stone to be repaired, an assessment must be made to determine the type of stone and where it is broken.

The most common type of breakage occurs at the base of the stone. Many forces combine at this level to create excessive stresses. If the gravestone has begun to tilt toward its front or back, constant pressure is being exerted and the weight of the stone acts like a lever. The taller the stone, the greater the forces will be; the thinner the stone, the more likely it will snap.

Historically, such breakages were often repaired by simply puddling the gravestone into concrete. A hole was dug, which was then filled with concrete. The gravestone was then stuck into the puddle. This technique is no longer recommended as it makes future preservation efforts difficult or impossible.

Another method was to simply reset the gravestone in a lowered position. This may be the quickest method and even a reasonable temporary measure. In order to safely reset the stone, at least one-third of it must be buried. However, this requirement may create problems with the inscription, as some or most of it may have to be buried.

A good gravestone conservation method is explained in detail on the Association For Gravestone Studies website, **www.gravestonestudies.com**. A replacement base is cast with a socket and the gravestone is set in place with a high-lime concentrated mortar. With this method, uneven breaks must be trimmed away and the underground portion of the stone must be removed if it is to be reset in the same location.

Advice for Mending Stone with Epoxy

The most common causes of epoxy repair failure can be avoided by following a few guidelines:

- **Wear gloves** when working with all epoxies.
- **All fragments to be joined must first be thoroughly cleaned and dried** before any epoxy can be applied to the mating surfaces. Also, be very careful to **apply the epoxy to only one of the mating surfaces** without spreading it too close to the edge. This will prevent any excess epoxy from being squeezed out onto the surface. (Excess epoxy can be removed with a solvent before it hardens, but this can also weaken the joint.)
- **Make sure the stone is dry**. A propane torch may be used to quickly evaporate moisture in cooler weather. Pass the torch back and forth quickly, so as to not heat one spot. Most stones will lighten in color as they dry, so this is a good indicator.
- **If the stone is too cold, the epoxy will not cure properly**. It may be wise to let the sun warm up a stone during cooler weather. If rain or cold weather is in the forecast, consider waiting until a fairer day to complete an epoxy repair. *The majority of epoxy repair failures are caused by cold, moisture or poor surface preparation.*

CAUTION: This chapter presents general recommendations that, while field tested, may not apply in all circumstances. Be careful to identify the material from which a particular marker is made before attempting to clean, repair or alter it in any way. The publisher and author offer no guarantees of outcome and accept no responsibility for damage that may incur using these suggestions. Proceed according to your own judgment and at your own risk.

CHAPTER 6

TAKING

RUBBINGS

Taking a rubbing is the practice of ...

... making a relief impression of lettering, carving or designs from a gravestone using paper and other materials.

Rubbings create a useful record of family information, sometimes becoming the only permanent reproduction of gravestones that have deteriorated over time. Popularized by the Chinese thousands of years ago, gravestone rubbing is popular today with folklorists and genealogists. However, this technique has fallen out of favor with many conservationists and preservationists, as rubbing can potentially damage a gravestone. Most experts allow that only one rubbing will not do any harm, but repeating the procedure can break down the sharp edges of the carved letters and numbers, allowing water to penetrate. This leads to a pattern of freezing and thawing, which can eventually so damage a stone that it will be illegible.

Knowing the correct way to handle rubbing materials and the gravestones themselves will help to preserve these markers for future generations. It is also important to keep in mind that many cemeteries have outlawed the practice, so it is best to check with the cemetery superintendent and to respect their rules. Always remember when working with a gravestone to do no damage.

Suggested Materials

Paper - Butcher paper, newsprint, vellum tissue or pellon (interfacing material) are recommended. Most rubbings are done on white paper with a dark wax or crayon, but experiments with darker papers and light or metallic waxes may reveal dramatic results. Some monument makers sell a blue paper covered with wax or even a rubbing kit. Blank newsprint is also good, but it tears easily. Pellon is the most widely available and the least expensive material, coming in various colors and weights.

Crayon or wax - The preferred media are lumber crayons or rubbing wax; chalk or charcoal can also be used, but each requires spraying the finished rubbing with a fixative (sold at most art stores) to prevent smearing. A very good and inexpensive rubbing wax is to take a box of crayons, remove their wrappers and meld them in a coffee can filled with several inches of hot water. Then, pour the contents into an old pie tin lined with paper or aluminum foil for cooling. Once hardened, break or cut into usable pieces.

Small, soft, slanted paintbrush - This is essential to clean debris and critters out of lettering and carvings.

Small, natural bristle brush - Use this to clean lichen and bird droppings off the stone's face.

Assorted plastic scrapers - These come in handy to help clean moss, lichens, etc. from the gravestone. Cheap scrapers work better than more expensive ones, as they are usually softer and will not damage the stone. Flat, wooden craft sticks are also useful to have on hand for scraping.

Tape - Unfortunately, all types of tape will leave some residue on the gravestone. However, drafting and painter's tape are less sticky and are, therefore, better for taking rubbings. Masking tape, duct tape and package tape will leave an excessive amount of glue, which will be difficult to remove from the stone and the completed rubbing.

Cardboard tube - This is useful for storing both clean paper and finished rubbings.

Pencil and notepad - This is essential for recording information about the stone and the cemetery itself.

CAUTION: Remember that doing rubbings often requires you to be on private property. It is always advisable to obtain permission to do rubbings from the owner before you begin. Some inexperienced and careless folklorists have done serious damage to gravestones and, for this reason, many cemeteries do not permit rubbings of any kind. If you do not receive permission, respect the wishes of the cemetery and instead take a photograph to record the information and condition of the gravestone. If you find that a gravestone is severely damaged, please notify the superintendent of the cemetery.

Additional Tips and Optional Equipment

- Bring scissors to cut paper or trim tall grass round the base of the stone, which is often where much wonderful text is hidden on old stones.

- An old towel comes in very handy to kneel on or to use in cleaning granite stones.

- Use a small pail to carry supplies or water for cleaning.

- Wear a hat; use sunscreen and bug repellent.

- Carry a sample size of antibacterial waterless hand cleaner or towelettes.

- Bring a small spray bottle of water.

- Use a scrap of leather to buff the rubbing for a softer effect before removing it from the gravestone.

- Don't forget your camera!

Rubbing Procedure

Be sure to choose a stone that is smooth, undamaged and cleanly carved. If the stone has begun to peel or flake, rubbing can easily cause more damage. The best choices are polished granite or intact, solid slate. Lightly rap on the stone. If it has a hollow sound, do not use the monument to take a rubbing, as it will be vulnerable to damage.

Before taping the paper to the gravestone, write any essential information on or about the monument (inscription, date, location, etc.) on the back of the paper. Completing this prior to taking the rubbing will ensure that the final image is not smeared. (Alternatively, record the information in a notebook, later detaching the page and including it with the completed rubbing.)

Tape the paper to the surface securely and smoothly. Make sure that it not only covers the sides, but also extends beyond the edges and top of the stone to avoid making any marks off the paper.

Determine the edges of the carved areas by filling in the outside boundaries. Then, move to the center using the broad, flat surface of the wax or crayon, making gentle, even strokes. More definition can be added later. Keep the strokes uniform in pressure to avoid coloring variations.

Step back a couple of times in order to determine if you have completely rubbed all the areas before moving the paper.

Carefully remove the rubbing, roll it and place it in the cardboard tube to protect it from tearing. Be sure to remove all tape from the stone and police the area for any remaining debris.

Some people proudly display their gravestone rubbings by mounting and framing them. Adding a title with the family name and location of the rubbing can make for an interesting conversation piece.

Glossary of Gravestone Elements and Cemetery Vocabulary

Abrasive - Media used to inscribe modern monumental works. May be composed of aluminum oxide, silicon carbine, steel shot, etc. Can also be sand or powdered pumice stone, which is rubbed against a sculpture's surface to create a smooth or polished effect.

Acid Rain - Rainfall with a lower than normal pH.

Acidic Deposition - Acid rain fallen on an absorbent stone is the leading cause of damage and decay to calcium carbonate-based rock, including most marble and some limestone.

Aggregate - Inert granular material, such as sand, gravel, crushed stone, slag, pumice and scoria that are mixed with water and cement to make mortar or concrete.

Arch - A curved construction that spans an opening.

Architrave - Member of an entablature that rests on the capitols of columns or piers to support a frieze.

Argillaceous - Consisting of or containing clay.

Armature - Internal frame or hidden support.

Artificial Stone - Simulated stone composite material.

Ashlar - Angled patterns in a straight line of stonework.

Ashlar Block - A squared or rectangular block of building stone that is set face-bedded; often incorporated into facades of mausoleums, crypts and historic masonry structures.

Assemblage - Sculptural form made by assembling various shapes and materials.

Assessment - Determines the condition of an object.

Atmospheric Staining - Deposition of particulate matter such as soot.

Atmospheric Incrustation - A surface crust formed by a reaction between calcium and acidic water to form calcium sulfate.

Backfill - The operation of replacing dirt removed in excavation.

Baluster - Series of miniature columns (or other form of upright piers) supporting a railing or handrail.

Barrow - Mound of stones or dirt on top of a grave.

Basalt - A dark, dense volcanic rock; difficult to shape.

Base Coat - Scratch coat; first layer of infill.

Bead - A jutting horizontal protrusion near the top of a decorative pillar.

Bed - Flat surface of a stone parallel to its stratification.

Bed Joint - Horizontal layer of mortar on which a masonry unit is laid.

Biological Activity - Algae or lichen growth visible on the stone's surface.

Blind Pinning - To place hidden support in a structure or monument in order to join sections together; may be employed during construction or as a repair technique (pinning should be of a non-ferrous metal or fiberglass material).

Blistering - Spalling of the second degree.

Block - A concrete masonry unit made with fine aggregate and cement shaped in a mold.

Bluestone - A hard, fine-grained stone often used for walkways or patios.

Bond - The property of a hardened mortar that knits the masonry units together.

Border Design - Carving that often ornaments the side panels of historic tablet stones.

Boxed Column - A supporting column that is square-shaped as opposed to circular; most often found on a Doric capital.

Box Tomb - A crypt-style monument with no body interred inside; the interior is a hollow cavity.

Brass - Alloy of copper and zinc that is malleable and stronger than copper.

Brick Masonry - Type of construction that has units of baked clay or shale of uniform size and is small enough to be placed with one hand and laid in courses with mortar joints to form walls, pillars and various structures.

Brick Set - Wide-blade chisel used for cutting bricks and blocks.

Bronze - Alloy of approximately 90 percent copper and 10 percent tin containing small amounts of other metals such as lead and zinc; hard and durable; commonly used for sculptural works.

Brown Coat - The second coat of stucco in a three-coat work.

Brownstone - Also known as sandstone; can be reddish, light brown, blond and dark brown; found throughout New England.

Burial - To place in the ground.

Burial Mound - A mound resulting from dirt piled upon a corpse.

Burial Vault - Concrete or other material used as a grave liner to keep a grave from subsiding.

Butter - To apply a quantity of mortar onto a brick, block or stone, often on the small end, prior to it being laid.

Buttress - Often associated with Gothic architecture, this is the out-jutting (thickening) of a wall to support an overhead beam or roof arch.

Cairn - A mound of stones serving as memorial or marker.

Calcareous - Consisting of or containing calcium carbonate or carbonate of lime.

Calcining - Burning; enough heat to cause disintegration or total fusion.

Calcite - A rock-forming mineral, calcite is found in limestone and seashells; very common on the earth's surface, as it dissolves in water and grows anywhere that water can reach.

Calcium - A soft, silver-white chemical element found in limestone, marble and chalks.

Caliper - Measuring instrument that has two movable parallel jaws that can be set in place in order to determine a specific size.

Cap - The top cement surface on a masonry structure.

Capital - The upper-most member of a column or pilaster; often supports an architrave or entablature, and is usually decorated.

Capstone - Stone atop a monument or wall.

Carving - Traditional subtractive method of producing a sculpture in which the material is cut or chipped away; also a term used to describe setting an inscription or decoration in a gravestone or monument.

Casket - A rectangular coffin.

Cast - Form produced by filling a mold.

Cast Iron - Iron object made in a mold.

Catacomb - An underground cemetery with tunnels and chambers where graves are placed.

Caulk - To seal up crevices with flexible material.

Cavity Wall - A wall with an air space behind it, such as in a box tomb.

Cement - Binding material that holds the aggregates together in concrete and mortar, curing into a
solid mass; derived from the Latin *caedere* ("to cut"), it signifies a substance to adhere objects.

Cemetery - Final resting place for human remains; larger, planned and more organized (park-like) in
structure than the earlier graveyards and burying grounds.

Cenotaph - Greek for "empty tomb"; monument to honor a person who is buried elsewhere or
whose body was never found.

Chasing - The final process of finishing a bronze cast once it has cooled from the furnace; chisels and
punches are used to remove imperfections, and the surface is polished or smoothed down.

Charnel House - Place for storing bones or corpses.

Chatoyancy - Silky appearance on the surface of a mineral; known as "cat's eye" effect.

Chamfer - Beveled surface formed by cutting a 45 degree angle from a squared edge or corner surface.

Chisel - Steel tool used for shaping stone, wood or metal; often held at an angle and struck with a mallet
to force the sharp, cutting edge along the surface being carved.

Clasts - Fragments in sedimentary rocks that originally formed parts of other rocks.

Claw Chisel - A chisel with its cutting edge divided into two or more prongs.

Clay - Malleable, moist earth mixed with water that becomes hard when baked.

Cleavage - The way a mineral breaks along a plane according to its atomic structure. In rocks, the way it
splits along the bedding planes or striations.

Closure Brick - A partial brick that is cut to fit into a place to complete a course.

Coffin - Box in which a body is laid to rest.

Colonnade - A row of columns.

Coloring Agents - Colored aggregates or iron oxides ground finer than the cement.

Columbarium - A vault with niches for urns containing human ashes.

Column - A tall, vertical, cylindrical member, most often associated with a classical capitol.

Come-Along - A ratcheted hand winch.

Composite Stone - Artificial stone formulated to match existing substrate in stone conservation.

Compressive Strength - The power to resist crushing under pressure. (Contrasted with tensile strength, the power to resist the action of forces pulling apart.)

Concrete - Artificial "stone" made by mixing cement and sand with gravel, broken stone or other aggregate. These materials must be mixed with sufficient water to cause the cement to set and bind the entire mass. Concrete is the preferred material for all modern monument foundations.

Conservation - Conserving, saving and protecting what exists; stabilizing what is left of an artifact.

Consolidation - The process whereby a weakened stone is treated to strengthen and prolong its lifespan.

Coping - Large stone blocks set at the perimeter of a gravesite; most often found on large Victorian family plots; the top course of a masonry wall.

Corbel - A horizontal course of masonry projecting past the last course and supporting the course above; a self-supporting projection.

Corinthian - The most ornate of the three Greek orders; formed with a bell-shaped capital, two rows of Acanthus leaves and a detailed cornice.

Cornice - A decorative molding such as at the top of a window, ceiling or exterior wall; the uppermost section of the entablature.

Course - One of the continuous horizontal layers or rows of masonry that form a structure.

Crazing - The checking (cracking) of the surface of artificial stone, concrete, etc.

Creekstone - Smooth, rounded quartzite stone worn by water.

Crypt - Subterranean vault used as a burial chamber; may be located beneath a church floor.

Curing - The hardening of epoxy or resin; the process of protecting masonry against moisture loss during the early stages of setting.

Darby - A large float of metal or wood used to smooth freshly poured concrete.

Death Mask - Cast made of the deceased's face just after death.

Delimitation - Separation of stone layers along its bedding planes.

Dentils - A series of small square-toothed or block-like projections usually found below a pieces of molding; most commonly associated with Greek revival and Colonial revival structures.

Descanos - Roadside crosses, often found on alongside sharp bends in roadways.

Dissolution of Marble - Very advanced stage of deterioration; a combination of multiple decay mechanisms including, erosion, sugaring and spalling.

Dolomite - Geologically, a name for a carbonate rock that consists predominantly of this compound; as a mineral component, it is found it certain crystalline schists and in beds of gypsum.

Dolomitic Limestone - Limestone containing 10% to 80% mineral dolomite.

Doric - The simplest and most basic of the three Greek orders; associated with thick columns and a capital with a flat bowl below a block. This column does not stand on a base.

Dress - To shape a stone finely to fit in place.

Dressed Stone - The stone in masonry, after it has been squared with a hammer and chisel.

Dry-Stack - Stonework with mortar recessed so that it is invisible.

Dry Stone Wall - A stone wall built without mortar.

Efflorescence - The white or grayish crust sometimes formed on the surface of masonry or stone, often as calcium sulfate; caused by the leeching-out of soluble chemical salts from the stone or brick and mortar joints through the forces of capillary action and evaporation.

Embalm - To preserve a corpse; injecting chemicals to prevent decay. (Until modern embalming began after the American Civil War, it was almost impossible to transport the deceased any great distance. Thus, most people were buried in or near the town where they expired.)

Embellish - To add ornament; to adorn.

Emery - A grayish-black mineral used as an abrasive; emery cloth is a fine sandpaper.

Empirical - Based on practical, scientific experience.

Engraving - Inscription or image formed by carving or sandblasting into stone.

Entablature - Greek revival style; horizontal group composed of three members held up by columns. From lowest to highest in a structure, the three members include the architrave, frieze and cornice.

Entomb - To place in a tomb or grave.

Epitaph - Inscription on a gravestone or monument, often a short poem, literary piece or description of the deceased; very common on historic gravestones, but seldom used on modern monuments.

Erosion - The gradual wearing away of a stone's surface through the forces of temperature, wind, water and ice; often associated with "sugaring" in marble.

Evaporate - To change into or pass off in vapor; an important part of the rising damp cycle in gravestones, the force that pulls salts and minerals towards the surface of stone and masonry structures combined with capillary action.

Excavate - The process of digging out or around something.

Exfoliation - Peeling or scaling of the stone's surface.

Exhume - To remove from a grave.

Face - The front or inscribed surface of a gravestone or monument.

Failure - Collapse, rupture or fracture; in gravestones, it usually refers to a breakdown of a previous repair procedure.

Fallen - Memorial or sculpture that has toppled over onto the ground.

Fat - Cement brought to the surface by floating the slab.

Fat Mortar - A very sticky mortar due to the lack of sand.

Feather - Metal spacer used with wedges in drilled holes to crack apart stone.

Feldspar - One of the crystalline minerals in granite.

Ferrous Pinning - Metal that rusts and expands was used extensively in historic monumental installations. It has contributed to a host of problems, including cracking, staining, stone degradation and complete collapse.

Fieldstone - Rough, uncut stones picked from a field.

Figurative - Sculpture or art form in which figures or objects are displayed; most sculptural works found in cemeteries are figurative.

Finial - Image inscribed at a monument's shoulder area (top upper sides); most common on historic tablet stone.

Flaking - Minor delimitation of surface; a form of spalling; usually followed by blistering and scaling in successive order of severity.

Float - A wooded tool used to finish a concrete or masonry surface.

Fluorescence - Optical effect whereby a mineral appears to be a different color in ultraviolet light than in ordinary daylight.

Flute - A groove or channel cut or carved as an architectural decoration; most commonly placed as parallel grooves on an Ionic column.

Foliations - Patterns caused by aligned crystals in metamorphic rocks.

Footing - Foundation; base for a wall or other structure that provides stability; may be concrete or built masonry.

Footstone - Smaller gravestone set at the foot of a grave, most often in conjunction with a headstone; may be inscribed with only initials or names.

Form - Used to shape concrete, as in the construction of a replacement base to reset a broken stone.

Foundation - A base that supports a structure. In monuments, poor quality foundations (or none at all) account for a large percentage of structural failures.

Fragment - A piece of a broken gravestone, monument or sculpture.

Frieze - The middle horizontal member as found in classical entablature. The architrave is located below the frieze and the cornice is above.

Frost Line - Maximum depth to which frost normally penetrates the soil during the winter; depth varies from area to area depending on regional climates. (For example, in Kentucky the frost line is about 18 inches below the surface of the ground.)

Furrowing - Striking a V-shaped trough in a bed of mortar.

Fusion - The melting of minerals at extremely high temperatures.

Gable - The upper vertical triangular section of the end of a building having a double-sloped roof.

Gneiss - Hard, course-grained metamorphic rock known as a type of granite; composed of mica, quartz and schist, with additional iron, magnesium and silicates.

Gradation - The distribution of particle sizes, from course to fine, in a given sample of aggregate.

Grade - Slope of the ground around a gravestone, monument or structure.

Grade Line - The point at which a stone enters the ground; the most common site of tablet stone breakage.

Granite - An igneous rock made up of mica, quartz and feldspar; predominant stone used in American monuments during the 20th Century. Most modern monuments and footstones are composed of granite, which is now imported in a wide range of colors from around the world.

Granular Disintegration - The final and most advanced stage of marble or limestone decomposition exhibiting extensive sugaring and erosion with lost inscriptions; a highly weakened and deteriorated stone.

Grave - A place of burial.

Grave Marker - Something placed in remembrance of the dead; the universal name to describe many types of memorials.

Gravestone - A stone placed on a grave to mark it, commonly inscribed with name, birth and death dates; most often describes an historic memorial and tends to mean a monolithic (one-piece) stone such as a tablet stone.

Gauging - Stirring or mixing.

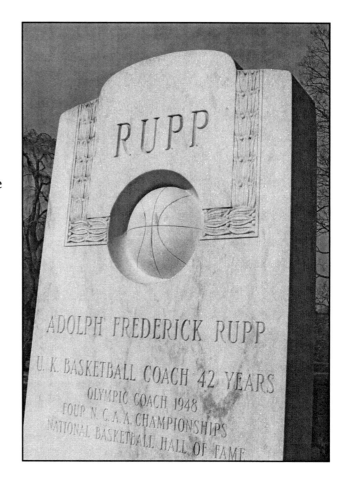

Granolithic - Consisting of artificial stone with a fine granular structure.

Grout - Thin mortar used in almost liquid consistency to fill joints or cavities.

Gypsum - Mineral consisting of the hydrous sulphate of calcium; used to make plaster of Paris.

Gypsum Crust - Calcareous stone sometimes degrades to form a highly decomposed incrustation on its outer surface in areas protected from rainfall; if removed, crumbling stone is likely underneath.

Hardening - Setting of concrete or mortar that may continue for months or years.

Hawk - A fairly small board with a handle beneath it that is used for holding mortar.

Header - A masonry unit laid flat with its longest dimensions perpendicular to the face of the wall; generally used to tie two widths of masonry together.

Headstone - A stone set at the head of a grave.

Hipped Roof - A roof that slopes downward from the peak on all four sides of a building.

Historic Pointing Mortar - Softer mortar designed for historic preservation containing a low percentage of Portland cement, such as a 1-4-8 (1 part Portland, 4 parts hydrated lime, 8 parts sand, by volume). It may contain natural cement, or can be a pure lime mortar, with no cement present.

Hydration - Chemical reaction that occurs when water is added to cement, causing it to harden.

Hydraulic - Active in the presence of, or under the influence of, water (example: hydraulic cement hardens under water). Derived from the Greek *hudor* ("water").

Igneous Rock - Rock formed as molten magma cools and hardens under ground; granite is the most common example. (Course-grained igneous rock is called granite and is preferred for monuments and building facades.)

Immurement - To enclose, confine or entomb within walls.

Incised Carving - Decorative image or inscription cut into stone.

Incipient - Beginning to develop; in initial stages.

In-fill - Replacement compound; to patch or repair areas of lost or decayed stone, concrete or masonry.

Injection Grout - Very thin grout that is injected or otherwise fed into cracks or voids.

Interment - Burial.

Inscription - Lettering carved or sandblasted into a gravestone or monument.

In-Situ - On site; constructed or conserved in position.

Ionic - The second of the three classical Greek orders; column designed by the Ionic Greeks; characterized by a spiral scroll called a volute.

Iridescence - A play of colors on the surface of a mineral, like a film of oil on water.

Joint - Any place where two or more edges or surfaces come together.

Keystone - The top stone in an arch or the center stone in a flat span.

Lamination - A protective thickness built up in layers.

Laminated Stone - Built up in layers when formed, such as sandstone.

Lancet Windows - Tall, narrow Gothic windows characterized by sharply pointed tops.

Leaded Glass Windows - A window having small panes of glass held in place by lead. Assorted decorative shapes were often combined with clear, etched, stained and beveled glass. Commonly associated with church buildings; were often incorporated into mausoleums of the very wealthy.

Ledgestone - Pattern of stonework utilizing horizontal joints.

Lime - Produced by burning limestone in a kiln; the base for mortar.

Limestone - A sedimentary rock formed from shells and organic sea matter. If metamorphosed, it becomes marble. Limestone was often used in 19th Century monuments as a base. May be difficult to distinguish from marble, but tends to be grayer in color than the originally white marble.

Lintel - A horizontal support for masonry; a stone spanning an opening; a horizontal beam over a door or window that carries the weight of the wall above.

Lunette - Semi-circular tympanum (upper center area on some gravestones); may contain an image such as a cherub, urn and willow, or death's head.

Luster - The way a mineral shines as affected by light reflecting off its surface.

Magma - Molten rock beneath the Earth's surface.

Mantle - A shelf built into masonry for decoration.

Marble - Metamorphosed limestone; predominantly used during the Victorian era for gravestones, monuments and sculpture. It is most sought after in its purest white form of calcium carbonate (unfortunately, also the stone most affected by acid rain).

Masonry - Anything constructed of the materials stone, brick, block, concrete, tile and mortar.

Mausoleum - Large, elaborate tomb or building to hold human remains.

Medallion - A decorative plaque with slightly projecting carvings.

Metamorphic Rock - Rock formed or changed by heat and compression. Examples include limestone becoming marble, shale becoming slate, and some sandstones becoming quartzite.

Metamorphism - The action of heat and pressure.

Memorial - Stone commemorating a person; may or may not be marking a grave site (example: for a ship captain lost at sea, a gravestone would have been placed at the site without a body).

Mend - To join broken fragments.

Mica - Mineral that occurs in thin sheets and tends to sparkle; a major component of granite.

Mineral - A solid mixture of chemicals that have certain regular characteristics, such as atomic structure and chemical composition.

Mineral Vein - Cracks in rocks that become filled with hot, mineral-rich liquids during their formation.

Missing Gravestone - Buried or disintegrated stone, unfound in a previously documented location.

Mohs Hardness Scale - A scale devised by the Austrian mineralogist Friedrich Mohs that measures the hardness of mineral by scratching. Scale ranges from one to ten, with talc ranked softest at number one and diamond designated a ten in terms of hardness.

Mold - A negative form, from which a cast is made.

Monolith - A term applied to a single piece of work, such as a one-piece gravestone or monument. Derived from a word of Greek origin, its literal meaning is "one stone."

Monument - From the root word meaning "to think"; a building, structure or memorial; a headstone constructed of two or more sections; can include a wide range of types and styles.

Mortar - A plastic mixture of lime and sand, with other possible ingredients such as horse hair; used chiefly for bonding masonry units together. Portland cement is a modern mortar.

Mud - Mortar.

Natural Bed - The surface of a stone, parallel to its stratification.

National Historic Landmark - America's highest designation for historic structures instituted by the Roosevelt Administration in 1935.

National Register of Historic Places - America's official list of buildings, sites and districts that includes some cemeteries; founded by Congress in 1966 but administered by states.

Necropolis - A city of the dead; a cemetery, especially a large extensive one, in an ancient city.

Oolith - Small, rounded grains that make up some sedimentary rocks.

Order - The three Greek orders included Doric, Ionic, and Corinthian. Each symbolized a specific style of column, capital and entablature. Sometimes the orders were interchanged or combined in the same structure.

Ore - Rock or other material from which a metal is extracted.

Parapet - In an exterior wall, the part entirely above the roof.

Patching Compound - Composite mixture to infill lost stone.

Patina - Final surface texture or color; protective crust that forms over time on the surface of some types of stones.

Pavers - Bricks in numerous sizes and shapes used for constructing sidewalks, patios and driveways.

Pediment - Triangular, gabled end of the roof that is above the horizontal cornice.

Perfect Cleavage - Property of mineral that breaks only in certain directions.

Perpetual Care - Guarantee of eternal cemetery upkeep; funds are collected and set aside; sometimes markers are placed beside monuments, or inscriptions added to stones, to denote payment has been collected.

Pier - A very wide pillar; a free-standing column; a vertical stone column that supports structures; a section of masonry used to carry weight from above, as in an arch, beams or girders.

Pigment - Substance used as a coloring agent. Originally made from natural products, today pigments sometimes include synthetic materials and are often used in paints, dyes and for stone conservation to shade or color composite infill materials.

Pilaster - An attached pier or pillar, often with a capital and base; a pier built in a wall to strengthen against horizontal forces or for appearance.

Pillar - A column-like support without a classical capital.

Pitch - To use a chisel to square a stone.

Pitting - Distinct depressions on a stone's surface.

Plastic - Capable of being molded, formed, modeled or spread like a mortar or paste.

Plasticity Consistency - A sluggish flow without segregation.

Plinth - A block that raises a monument or sculpture.

Plinth Course - The projecting course of masonry often called the water table.

Plumb - Perfectly straight up and down; vertically perpendicular as measured with a spirit level or plumb bob.

Plumb Bob - A weight attached to a line used to establish a plumb point on a surface.

Plumb Line - To extend a line from the top to the bottom of a structure.

Pointing - The process of filling in joints by inserting mortar after masonry has set.

Pointing Trowel - A small trowel used for filling in small holes and for pointing up work.

Porcelain - The finest of all ceramics; retains its strength even when very thin. Photographs of deceased have been affixed to monuments in porcelain frames or lockets.

Portico - A monumental projecting porch with a roof supported by columns; most commonly found at the front entrance of an important building or structure.

Portland Cement - Cement most often used in modern construction to formulate concrete, mortar and pre-cast products. Creates a very hard solid; not recommended for most aspects of historic preservation.

Pre-cast Concrete - Any concrete member cast and formed at a place other than its final placement.

Preservation - To keep historic artifacts and objects safe from harm or injury for future generations.

Proportion - The correct or desirable relationship between parts.

Pry Bar - Tool used to lever or pry stone objects.

Pumice Stone - Volcanic stone, finely ground and used for polishing.

Punch - Pointed steel tool used like a chisel to remove chips or stone; historically, the "work-horse" of stone cutting.

Quartz - A common crystalline stone; major component of granite.

Quartzite - Metamorphic sandstone; harder, denser sandstone.

Quarry - A rock bed; a natural location from which rock is cut.

Rafter - A diagonal member that forms the shape and structure of a sloping roof and supports the roofing material.

Rake Joint - To remove some of the mortar from a joint to a uniform depth before it hardens.

Regauge - To remix mortar as it begins to harden to extend pot life; retemper.

Reinforcing Rod - Steel rod used for reinforcing concrete or masonry; rebar.

Relief - A design made to relieve a flat surface; can project or be incised.

Reset - Reinstallation of a leaning, fallen or damaged gravestone or monument.

Reset Lowered - A gravestone that has been reset in a lowered position due to being fractured near ground level.

Restoration - To restore or make new again. More aggressive than conservation, restoration implies recreating what has been lost.

Retaining Wall - A wall of masonry used to hold soil or other material in place.

Retemper - To stir thoroughly again so as to produce a workable consistency.

Revival Styles - Classical styles incorporated into new architectural works. Greek, Egyptian, Romanesque, etc., became very popular in America throughout the 19th and 20th centuries.

Riprap - Irregular stone used for fill or to hold against erosion.

Rising Damp - Moisture brought upwards through the forces of capillary action and evaporation.

Rock - Solid mixtures or aggregates of minerals.

Roof Ridge - The top horizontal member of a sloping roof.

Romanesque Revival - Roman and Byzantine styles characterized by their massive size; often included the rounded arch; popular during the second half of the 19th Century.

Rowlock - A brick laid on its edge or face.

Rubble - Rough fragments, either natural or broken stone, used in coarse masonry or as fill-in concrete or walls.

Running Bond - Same as common bond with continuous horizontal joints, but the vertical joints are offset or inline.

Sandstone - Sedimentary rock made of compressed sand; formed from fresh water sediment; used extensively in the form of brownstone in northeastern U.S. from the late 1600s to about 1900.

Sarcophagus - A stone coffin.

Scaling - The most advanced form of spalling.

Scarify - To make scratches in mortar or cement so the next coat has a stronger bond.

Schist - A metamorphic crystalline rock that easily splits along its bedding planes; used to create gravestones in some geographic locations.

Scratch Coat - The first coat in infill, stucco or plaster.

Screed - A long, very straight board used for striking off concrete.

Screeding - The process of leveling the surface of a concrete slab by striking off excess concrete.

Sedimentary Rock - Rock that forms at Earth's surface; consists of layers of rock fragments or other substances that have been deposited on top of each other (examples include lakes and riverbeds becoming sandstone or seabeds becoming limestone).

Segregation - The tendency of particles of the same size in a given mass of aggregate to join whenever the material is being loaded, transported or otherwise distributed.

Sepulcher - A burial vault; a place to store relics in an altar.

Setting - Installation of a new monument; the process during which mortar or concrete hardens. The initial set occurs when the concrete or mortar has to be broken in order to change its shape. Rate varies greatly depending on temperature, amount of sunlight and specific masonry mix.

Setting Bar - Steel bar formed as a round, square or octagonal shape; constructed from two to six or more feet long; used to lift, maneuver and handle heavy weights with a mechanical advantage through leverage; a monument is "set" by being dropped down off a setting bar.

Setting Clamps - Tool that is firmly attached onto a die stone, allowing the stone to be lowered without risk of chipping.

Setting Compound - Also known as monument setting compound, it is available in gray, dark gray, brown and white; the preferred material used to install new monuments.

Setting Cushions - A spacer placed between stone sections that may be composed of lead, plastic or other hard materials.

Shale - Thin-layered soft stone of clay origin that becomes slate if metamorphic.

Shim - Cushion or spacer placed between stone segments; may be lead, copper or plastic and vary in thickness.

Siliceous - Containing silica (examples: quartz, sand, sandstone).

"Shot" Stone - Stone quarried using explosives.

Shoulder - Upper outside corners on a gravestone.

Slate - Hard durable rock that comes from metamorphic shale composed mainly of clay; formed in layers and sometimes delaminates along its bedding planes. (Many of the oldest and best-preserved examples of colonial gravestones were carved from slate. These can be found throughout New England, especially in Boston.)

Slings - Constructed from polyester, nylon or other very strong material; the stone is hung from slings in order to be raised, moved or set.

Sling Bar - Tool that spreads slings apart, allowing monuments to be lifted.

Soapstone - A soft stone composed largely of talc; carves easily and is heat-resistant; tends to work more like wood than stone.

Soldier Course - A course of brick laid standing on edge with the thin side on the face.

Soul Effigy - Common symbol found on American gravestones from the mid-18th Century through the mid- to late 19th Century, then replaced largely by the Greek revival image of the urn and willow.

Soundness - Absence of a tendency to crack, swell, shrink, distort or disintegrate under varying conditions.

Spall - To flake or split away; indicates loss of stone.

Specific Gravity - Comparison of a mineral's weight with that of an equal volume of water.

Stabilize - To make safe or secure; to prevent from falling or being damaged.

Star Drill - Chisel-like drill that is struck with a hammer and turned, then struck again repeatedly to slowly create holes in stone.

Stele - A commemorative inscribed stone or sculpture set in the facade of a building; can serve as a gravestone.

Stone Point - Sharp, pointed chisel for finishing stone faces.

Streak - The color of a mineral's powder; often a more useful identification method than surface color because it gives less variable results.

Stretcher - A brick or block laid lengthwise in a wall.

Striations - One of a series of parallel stripes or lines; with rock, formed by veins of minerals joining, which may be considered blemishes or defects to be avoided.

Striking - Taking down or removing, as in the removal of forms.

Struck Joint - A joint made by pressing the mortar with a trowel.

Stucco - Cement mortar or gypsum plaster of two or more layers used to surface coat exterior or interior masonry walls or structures.

Sub Foundation - The first layer of material placed in excavated ground prior to the foundation; may be composed of crushed stone, cinders.

Survey - To examine a graveyard or cemetery in planning for preservation.

Symmetrical - Having the exact forms or masses on either side of a center line or plane.

Tablet stone - A single-piece vertical gravestone.

Table stone - A memorial composed of legs or a built masonry base supporting a large horizontal stone and usually containing an inscription.

Table tomb - Box tomb or crypt-style monument without a body inside; often represents a table with six legs.

Tamping - The act of pounding, packing or consolidating, as in working concrete or compacting dirt during backfill.

Tempering - Adding water to mortar in order to bring back a workable texture.

Tensile Strength - The holding power or measure of adhesiveness of concrete, masonry or stone; power to resist the action of forces tending to pull apart. (Contrasted with compressive strength, the power to resist crushing under direct pressure.)

Texture - The tactile and visual quality of a surface, regardless of its color.

Texturing - Creating a particular finish, such as brushed, smoothed, etched or pockmarked.

Tie-Stone - A long stone that extends across a wall.

Tomb - A grave, burial vault or a monument.

Tombstone - Gravestone; denotes historical type, often within the western United States.

Tower - A tall structure, most often round or square, rising from the ground to a height above its entire surroundings.

Tracery - Curving bars that form a decorative shape within a Gothic window.

Transom - An opening over a door or window, most often for ventilation; contains a glazed or solid sash that is usually hinged or pivoted.

Trap Rock - A dark-colored igneous rock of great weight and strength, including basalt, feldspar, etc.

Treatment - Performing conservation procedures.

Trowel - A steel tool with a flat surface for buttering, spreading and smoothing mortar or concrete; produced in various shapes and sizes with specific names for each purpose.

True Up - To make level or plumb.

Tuck Pointer - A long, flat masonry tool made in varying widths from a quarter to half an inch.

Tuck Pointing - Filling the joints in masonry with mortar using a tuck pointer.

Tumulus - Burial mound or barrow.

Turret - A corner tower that rises from the second floor or roof line.

Tympanum - The semi-circular upper section (lunette) on some tablet stones.

Unstable - A hazardous or dangerous gravestone, monument or structure that may be in danger of toppling or falling apart.

Urn - Container for ashes of a person who has been cremated.

Vaulted Ceiling - A ceiling formed from a continuous arch that is found in Roman, Classical and Gothic architecture and revival styles; a common technique employed in the 19th and 20th centuries for the construction of crypts and vaults in cemeteries.

Veneer - A layer of bricks, stones or other material that serves as a facing or outer surface.

Vitrify - To make glass-like (e.g., vitrified clay, glazed surfaces, etc.); usually completed by heating to the point of fusion.

Voids - Air space created from the movement or decomposition of stone or between particles or aggregates in a concrete or mortar.

Volute - A spiral scroll forming the major element of an Ionic capital.

Weathering - The breaking down of rocks or masonry by the action of various processes such as freezing and thawing and dissolving in water.

Wedges - Stone chips used for leveling; metal tools used in conjunction with feathers to split stone.

Stories

I walk among these still, gray stones –
moss covered, sun warmed to my hand –
reading names of established kinship
sounding as a litany down the ages,
and I am somehow comforted
knowing that I, too, one day shall sleep
among these storied stones
and that in the telling and retelling of my story
I, too, shall be remembered.

GAYLORD COOPER

CPSIA information can be obtained at www.ICGtesting.com
Printed in the USA
BVOW05s1137121213

338821BV00003B/21/P